MW00366701

Divorce can be scary and overv
Even when you consider yours
who knows what she wants an
make you question everything – who you are, what you want and
what's going to happen next. Feel familiar? *How to be a Lady
Who Leaves* is for you...

Emma Heptonstall's book is a crash course in divorce – all you
need to know but were afraid to ask.

The book is highly readable and jam-packed full of useful tactics,
tips and advice spanning the nuts and bolts of the legal process,
understanding your finances and how to successfully put your
children at the centre of your divorce.

Relying on the advice of your lawyer, friends and family is good
but having The Divorce Coach on your side is priceless. It's
important that you think strategically and logically and that you
keep emotion out of your decision-making as much as possible.
Every woman needs to understand (even if she is happily married)
what it takes to be a lady who leaves.

Jane Wintringham,
retired solicitor, divorcée, www.adelwills.co.uk

Divorce is so EMOTIONAL. That's why working with Emma prior
to and at the same time as having a family solicitor engaged has
been essential. And for both my soon-to-be-ex-husband and I,
those emotions (and where they are on the ever-changing scale
of defensive/angry/jealous/hurt/scared/confused/over-whelmed,
vulnerable etc) are precisely what drive a lot of the behaviours
which then feed into the legal process.

And so, you need to address these first, not run to either your solicitor or your mum, neither of whom can give you the actual help you need to *sort the emotions out first*, allow you some time to digest and settle them, and give you some accurate understanding and options as to how you might move forward in a way which will work for you.

This is where Emma is so invaluable. She specialises in ALL the areas on the painful separation and divorce journey. She is a qualified and experienced family lawyer, mediator, counsellor and an all-round fantastic woman. She gets it. All of it. She doesn't judge you, she supports, advises and cares. She'll laugh with you. This is exactly what you need on the painful and long separation and divorce 'one of the most stressful things you can go through' journey. (She is also much cheaper to cry to than your solicitor!)

The legal bit is essential of course, but actually, in itself, it's a smaller part of the whole route.

For example, ... you really intend to work things out sensibly with your ex. Children arrangements, in-law interference, who lives where, money, financial arrangements for the transition period and future, everything. You know that this is the sensible way and you certainly don't want massive and unnecessary legal fees, a dragged-out court process or indeed the stress and more upset that all that entails.

However! Your emotions (both yours and your ex's) are likely to be the key drivers in whether that goes reasonably well, or is a total nightmare.

» You have no idea what the legal process looks like, and you still hope to avoid or at least minimise it.
» You know solicitors are expensive but you're still horrified when you get the bill (and nothing is even 'happening' yet) and the irritation that they use old-fashioned letters rather

than a quick email, and the lack of certainty about whether you should try for Route A, Route B, Route C ... argh!

» You feel absolutely sick when either you or your ex have done the thing you swore you never would and said, "I'll see you in court then", as neither of you know what you meant by that, you just know that it seems a million miles off being resolved and sensible communications have (at least for now) broken down.

» You absolutely need to do the "you'll never guess what he did now / what his mother said / I can't get out of bed for crying today... am I normal" outburst, but you don't want to keep ON burdening your friends and family and you know that your solicitor is totally the wrong person too, but you just need to GET IT OUT!

» You know exactly what you want to happen one minute, you are in the dark and feeling terrified the next and you don't know what steps to take next either way.

In short, how you are feeling is a rollercoaster and most of us don't know how to do this stuff! Emma does. She gets it. She will get you. She feels like the best friend you wish you had on-tap, who you don't later have to feel embarrassed with. And the help and support she will give you for the whole thing is at least valuable, at best absolutely sanity-saving. And you can then use the (not cheap!) time with your solicitor to stay on-point and just get the legal part progressed with more clarity (and a much-reduced need for tissues).

Katie,
Lady Who Left

Emma has helped me in a way I will never forget. I am going through a lot of issues right now with my husband and my own personal family lawyer (my lawyer is not answering any of my questions or communicating with me at all and is making me feel like I'm bothering them). I reached out to Emma with questions regarding my case. She didn't once make me feel like I was bothering her, in fact, complete opposite! Because of her, I feel more relaxed and confident going forward with these issues. If you get the chance to work with Emma, PLEASE do not hesitate, her kind heart and open arms will ease you. Thank you again Emma.

Suzy,
Lady Who Left

Emma is a coach of exceptional skill. She has a proven ability to deliver transformative, life-changing 1:1 work with warmth, humour and integrity. Highly recommended.

Dr. Henrie Lidiard,
INLPTA Master Trainer

Dear Jules

Well, here we are!
At a book launch - when's yours
I hope I'm on the front row
cheering you on as you're
cheered me on.
Thank you f your friendship
and support.
Love,
Emma

How to be a

Lady Who Leaves

Printed in the United Kingdom

Illustrations by Lucy Monkman
www.lucymonkman.com

First Printing, 2017

ISBN: 978-0-9957390-4-8 (Print)
ISBN: 978-0-9957390-5-5 (eBook)

Librotas Books
Portsmouth, Hampshire, UK
www.LibrotasBooks.com

"People forget being in a relationship is a choice; I certainly did"

Katie

Contents

Foreword

Divorce is challenging. When it comes to ending a marriage and leaving, there can be a lot at stake. As a woman, your financial situation typically reduces by around 30%, and if you have children it drops even further. You may have to move out of your home, face a lengthy custody battle and/or pay exorbitant legal fees. To say nothing of the negative effects on your wellbeing, your health and your happiness as these dramatic changes in your life unfold.

You don't want to regret your decision. You need to be prepared. You need to be confident that your decision is right for you.

Getting divorced brings with it a whole raft of issues and figuring out how to deal with these egregious difficulties can be painful. What you really need is a hitchhiker's guide to point out the easier route – that 'must-have' reference book for any woman thinking of leaving.

Well, here it is. Open any page and you will find yourself a description of where you are at (wherever that might be), and a plan to help you move forward.

Emma Heptonstall, the author, has worked with hundreds of women who face the same difficult decision as you. A former lawyer and now a successful divorce coach, she has first-hand experience of the many difficulties that arise in divorce. Emma's acute awareness of her clients' emotional experience helps her to sensitively facilitate their journey. In her words, she has learned that "being a lady who leaves isn't easy. It requires courage, tenacity, bravery and confidence" but she also knows that you can do this and that you are reading this book because you need to explore this possibility.

Professionally, Emma and I share the same goals: to inspire and support women to live a happier and more fulfilled life. Through MeMeMe, my unapologetic online destination for women who desire more, talented wellbeing experts like Emma share their knowledge and experience to help women find greater clarity on what they want in their lives and to support them to make the necessary changes.

Like all our experts, Emma is making a huge and positive difference to women's lives. Through this remarkable book, she enables you to gain all the factual knowledge you require in an atmosphere of support and warmth. You won't find encouragement to leave but you will find the motivation to tune in and listen to your own voice.

Divided into seven sections, including the decision to leave, the divorce process in England and Wales, and life beyond your divorce, the book describes real-life case studies of women who came to Emma because they knew that leaving would be complicated financially and emotionally. Three women with different family situations and one common goal – to make a good decision for the right reason.

Behind the cold statistics of divorce are real people who, having started married life with love and optimism for the future, find themselves faced with a period of emotional malaise. *How to be a Lady Who Leaves* provides you with an easy to use toolkit to negotiate the legalities, but more than that, it offers the empathy that allows you to feel heard and focus your attention on the best outcome for yourself and your children without becoming warped by the bitter emotions of the tough situation you face.

You are in good hands.

Janet A. Hill
Founder and Editor of *MeMeMe*

Acknowledgements

I wanted to write books when I was 11 years old. That phase lasted a while and was followed by archaeologist, and then history teacher. It wasn't until I got to university that I realised I'd get eaten alive by a bunch of unenthusiastic teenagers and so I decided to become a lawyer instead.

After 13 years of working in crime and family law, family mediation and a career in coaching drew me away from being a lawyer – I guess I'll be in recovery forever, but mediating and coaching is where I belong.

This book is the culmination of years working with separating families in the legal arena, several years' experience as a family mediator, NLP Master Practitioner, Certified MBit Coach and working with my 1:1 clients, including the Ladies Who Left that you'll meet in this book. Angela, Katie and Yvonne, you are all amazing and your stories will go on to inspire others like you – thank you!

Thank you to my first business coach, Karen Williams, who has been by my side since the creation of Divorce Alchemy and who went on to support me as a book writing coach – I could not have written this book without you!

Thank you to David Brown; you taught me all I know about family law and how to deal with couples in a system not designed to support their emotional crisis.

Chris Myles, head of department and director at Crombie Wilkinson LLP York, where I still learn so much about being the best mediator I can be, thank you for reading the manuscript and sharing your thoughts and experience – I really appreciate it.

Thank you to Nina Farr, parenting leadership coach, for her support and for writing the section on domestic abuse – I thought such an important topic needed to be penned by an expert!

Lucy Monkman for the superb illustrations and bringing *Lady Who Leaves* to life – I adore her!

Thank you to the ladies who read the first draft of *How to be a Lady Who Leaves* – some of whom I knew and others not – I appreciate your time and the valuable and insightful feedback you gave me.

To my family and friends for their unwavering support, encouragement and excitement as *How to be a Lady Who Leaves* progressed: I love you all.

I also acknowledge you, the lady who leaves, for picking up this book. Even if you haven't truly acknowledged your thoughts to yourself yet, you picked up this book because you're curious.

It doesn't mean you will leave, but well done on being brave enough to journey with that thought – I hope this book supports you to take the steps that are right for you.

You can contact me via my website, follow me on Twitter, Instagram, like my Facebook page or join my groups on Facebook and LinkedIn:

www.emmaheptonstall.com
www.twitter.com/divorcealchemy
www.instagram.com/divorcealchemy
www.facebook.com/thedivorcealchemist
www.bit.ly/LadiesWhoLeave
www.bit.ly/LadieswhoLinkedin

You can also access additional resources and bonuses related to this book at:

bit.ly/Howtobealadywholeavesbookresources

Section 1

Are you a Lady Who Leaves?

Do you wish you could leave your marriage?

Be honest with yourself. Go on: it's just you and me. I'm guessing that you do, or you're thinking about it seriously because you've picked up this book!

Perhaps you've bought this book because you've decided to be a lady who leaves. Perhaps you've bought this book because you're not sure. I'll let you into a secret: lots of ladies just like you aren't sure. I've yet to work with a lady who flippantly decided to leave her husband. Leaving is a big decision. Leaving feels confusing, scary and a bit like failure. It's not what you envisaged when you got married. Making the right decision is important, isn't it? You want to know that you won't look back with regret. You want to know that leaving will be better than staying, even though you know the middle bit might not be a bed of roses.

This book will help you get clear on the decisions you need to make so that you can feel relaxed and confident that you are making a good decision. Being a lady who leaves isn't easy. It requires courage, tenacity, bravery and confidence (all the qualities you still have in bucket loads, by the way). I know that you're reading this book because deep down you do know you can do this (or at least you're willing to explore). That willingness and curiosity are just some of the skills you'll need on the way.

You'll want to know about the divorce process, how it works, the steps that you need to take, the timeframe and the likely outcomes. You'll want to know what will happen to your children, your finances and how to cope emotionally – I'll cover all of this in this book.

What if I decide not to leave?

You may be wondering what will happen if you decide you don't want to leave. Don't worry, this book is not designed to talk you into leaving. I will be signposting support for you if you decide that you'd like guidance on making your marriage work. You see, fundamentally, I believe in marriage – good marriage. When clients who work with me decide they don't want to leave, I celebrate them; my work is done. My wish for you is that this book gives you the clarity that you are looking for and it gives you the information and the tools you need to move forward.

The Divorce Alchemist

Am I a lady who has left?

No.

I haven't left because I'm not married ... yet. You may have picked up this book hoping to be able to learn from a lady who has been there, done that. Sorry, you won't find that story here. However, before you stick this book back on the shelf, hold on. It's because I'm not divorced that I am actually the best person to support you in deciding whether you should leave your husband, and given my background and professional experience, I am also the best person to support you with the decisions you need to make if you decide to divorce. You see, I know that in reaching out for this book, you want professional, impartial support. If you just wanted the advice of your friends, you'd still be getting it, wouldn't you?

Before my life as a divorce coach, I was a lawyer. I also now work as a family mediator. I've worked with hundreds of ladies navigating relationship breakdown. I know how scary, painful and confusing it is. I understand the mistakes that many ladies make. The mistakes that cost them financially and emotionally. So rather than my own subjective experience, this book is drawn on my objective, professional expertise. The stories I will share are those of the ladies that have been through the process of deciding to leave their husband and doing it. They are just like you. Once smart, confident and capable ladies, they felt like they'd lost who they were. The truth is, deep down they knew they could be that lady again, but only if they left.

Even if I had been divorced, I still wouldn't know what your divorce feels like – I'm not you. Your divorce is as unique as you and your marriage. This book is designed so that you can think about your situation. With your values, beliefs and hopes for the future. No two divorces are the same. Similar, yes. The same, no.

Who is this book for?

This book is for you if you are leaving (or thinking of leaving) your husband. You may also be in a same-sex relationship and if you're married, this advice will apply to you too. You feel alone, scared and confused about the decision to leave and its consequences.

How to be a Lady Who Leaves is for you if you have doubts about your decision or if you have made the decision and you need to know what your next steps are.

This book is for you if you want to move forward, make a decision and take action.

This book isn't about commiserating over a marriage that didn't work. For some ladies, leaving their marriage is something they want and embrace. It allows them to be the woman they want to be.

Not all marriages that end are 'bad' and not all ladies who leave feel like 'victims'. Sometimes for no particular reason, not because of any event or 'problem', marriages end.

It's important, even if this is you, that you deal with your separation and divorce appropriately from the start. Maintaining that amicable relationship you have is vital, but so is being smart. Don't assume because you wouldn't be underhand that at some point your husband won't be. Not because he's a bad person, but we all do crazy things when we're fearful. I worked with a lady who agreed with her husband to sell the family home. All the money went into his account. He didn't give her a penny and spent the lot. Did she get advice beforehand? No. Hindsight is a wonderful thing. It's often expensive.

This book is not for you right now if ...

This book is not for you right now if you are experiencing domestic abuse. Domestic abuse includes physical violence, emotional abuse and financial control. You may not even recognise that this is a feature of your relationship. See Section 2 on domestic abuse for further information and support.

This book is also not for you right now if your husband has recently left you and you are struggling emotionally. If you need counselling, seek that support from your GP. Coaching is not counselling. Coaching does not heal past wounds; rather its purpose is a solution focused future.

And lastly, this book is not for you if you want to wallow in self-pity and put off making a decision.

How to use this book

This book is written in seven sections. The first section is all about the decision to be a lady who leaves. I've yet to meet the lady who thought about leaving and just left. Leaving is a big decision and it's important that you are comfortable with that decision. The first section will explore that decision so that you can feel confident it's the right one for you. If you've already left, you may want to jump straight to the second section of this book and that's okay. However, you might want to check in with yourself by reading Section 1– the choice is yours!

Section 2 is written by leadership parenting coach Nina Farr, and is designed to give an overview of domestic abuse and sources of support.

The third section of this book is all about the divorce process in England and Wales – what you must do and when. It also contains information about court orders in relation to your finances and your children. Did you know that these are separate from your divorce proceedings? Many ladies are unaware of this.

All your divorce will do is legally end your marriage. That's it. It's quite straightforward. In reality, it's not the divorce itself that ladies struggle with; it's the decisions that need to be made about money and children which cause anxiety. The emotional turmoil that accompanies this, coupled with the sadness and anger of a 'failed marriage', are some of the things that ladies like you have challenges with.

Sections 4 and 5 deal with the biggest issues in separation and divorce – finances and children.

Sections 6 and 7 of this book look at the importance of taking care of yourself and life beyond your divorce. You will get there, you know!

This book contains lots of practical advice and information.

Legal information

Legal information is not the same as legal advice. Legal information is information about the law. For example, one of the major pieces of relevant legislation on divorce is **Section 25** of the **Matrimonial Causes Act 1973 (MCA 1973)**. This outlines the considerations the court will take into account when determining your financial settlement. Legal information would include details of what those considerations are, and how they work in practice (we will be looking at this later). Legal advice goes a step further. Legal advice consists of an explanation of the law, coupled with specific advice pertaining to your situation: "and so, Mrs Smith, my advice is that we argue/ask for [fill in the blank]". Only a practising lawyer is qualified and insured to give you this advice. You will not find legal advice in this book; you must seek that from your lawyer. I'll be sharing with you how to find a good lawyer later.

Case studies

Throughout this book, you will meet Angela, Katie and Yvonne. Angela is in her 50s; she has been married to Richard about 13 years and they have a young daughter. Katie, who is in her 40s, is married to Will – they have three children. They have been together since their late teens. Yvonne is in her 50s and has been married to Ted for over 20 years. They have two children.

As you might expect, the names of the clients mentioned in this book have been changed for confidentiality. All have generously allowed me to share their stories with you.

The thing that these ladies all have in common is that they are smart. They came to me because they recognised that even though they had thought about leaving their husbands, they knew it would be complicated both financially and emotionally. Making a good decision for the right reasons was important to them.

I will share with you some of the issues each of them faced and how together we explored these and how each of them moved forward. One of them is now divorced, one of them is going through the process, and one of them is separated but has not yet petitioned for divorce. I'm grateful to be able to share their stories with you and I hope that you find them useful.

You will also meet Rachel and Bob, clients I worked with in family mediation. I will briefly share their story and how family mediation changed their experience of divorce both emotionally and financially.

How this book will help you

This book will help you get clear about whether you want to leave. If you decide not to leave, I'll signpost you to support for you in your relationship. If you do decide to leave, this book will help you understand the legal process, your responsibilities, timeframes and costs. It is a companion for you to read and dip into as often as you like. It may help you to read the book through first at least once and then access relevant sections as you need them. I've included a glossary of legal terms to assist you and a list of useful organisations to support you. If you need my 1:1 support you can get in touch with me at emma@emmaheptonstall.com.

Finally…

Divorce is tough even when it is your idea, but remember, divorce is just a process, not a destination. Divorce doesn't say anything about you as a person. It is not related to your worthiness, or your value. Divorce is a process by which you can change your life because you're choosing something different. Let this book be your companion to keep you focused. A lady with knowledge and a plan will always fare better in divorce both emotionally and financially.

Thank you for letting me support you on your journey.

Emma

Meet the Ladies Who Left

Angela's story

Angela met and married Michael in her late 30s. Up until this point, Angela had been a successful career girl who liked to have fun. As she approached her mid 30s, Angela felt that she wanted to settle down and have children. She married Michael who was the complete opposite of her. Angela shared with me that her life with Michael was unfulfilling. Michael struggled with the fact that Angela was the main breadwinner, earning almost double his salary. He was also emotionally controlling and a bully. Although she was outwardly successful, Angela's self-esteem and confidence were at rock bottom.

Angela contacted me wracked with guilt that she was unhappy in her marriage and had begun a passionate affair with Richard, who was also going through divorce. Angela was confused because she didn't want to be a divorced woman, but her relationship with Richard had made her realise what was missing in her marriage. Her relationship with Richard was fun. It was full of laughter, playfulness and connection as well as great sex!

It's not that Angela hadn't tried working on her marriage. She and Michael had previously been to relationship counselling, but Michael refused to accept any responsibility for the issues in their relationship and wanted to blame Angela. From Angela's point of view, relationship counselling had not worked.

Angela wasn't sure if she wanted to leave Michael. She also wasn't sure if her relationship with Richard was too good to be true, or based on their mutual unhappiness in their relationships.

During our sessions together, Angela and I explored how leaving Michael and her relationship with Richard were, in reality, separate issues, and that by linking the two, she was causing her own confusion. As Angela began to separate the two issues out, she was able to focus fully on her relationship with Michael and to recognise that leaving Michael did not mean that she would have a relationship with Richard. She recognised that she could leave Michael and be single if that's what happened.

Katie's story

When Katie called me, she too was in a quandary about her marriage. Like Angela, Katie and her husband Will had been to relationship counselling. In fact, they'd been going for years. Whilst Will agreed to go after much persuasion by Katie, he was disengaged and nothing had changed.

Katie felt alone, frustrated and scared. The stress caused Katie significant health issues that had culminated in her hospitalisation for a period. Katie knew that things had to change, but she struggled with the sadness of the loss of her marriage, and worried about the impact upon the children, and upon her husband whom she still loved.

Katie, like Angela and Yvonne, is a strong, smart woman. Having put her career on hold to raise her youngest child who is still a toddler, Katie looked after the children, managed a family business and dealt with all the family finances whilst her husband was at work.

Katie is also what I would call a 'fixer'. Like many of the women I work with, Katie's husband Will suffered significant trauma as a child which is unresolved and causes emotional problems in his adult life. Katie recognises that these emotional issues are also a cause of many of the issues in their marriage. This has led Katie to minimise and excuse her husband's behaviour. Katie struggled to accept her husband was emotionally abusive and controlling. She feels desperately sad for him in spite of the pain that he causes her.

When Katie and I explored whether her marriage was truly over, Katie was repeatedly drawn to worrying about how her husband would cope emotionally and practically with life after the end of the marriage. For a few months, Katie struggled with the idea that separation and divorce would possibly be about saving herself from a marriage that had been destroying her for at least a decade.

Yvonne's story

Yvonne and Ted have been married for over 20 years. With two children in an expensive school, several homes and a complex financial portfolio, Yvonne felt trapped. By the time Yvonne called me, Ted was already aware that Yvonne was unhappy. Ted had also admitted that he was unhappy but believed the two of them should stay together because of his long-term financial plan. Ted believed that money was more important than being happy. This made Yvonne feel even more scared. Yvonne is a smart, intelligent woman. It has been her role in the family to raise the children and deal with their property portfolio. Ted has looked after all other financial investments, and made all the financial plans. Whilst Yvonne has not been prevented from accessing this financial information, neither has it been explained to her despite her requests. This is Ted's way of feeling in control. Even though Yvonne knows that there is enough money for the two of them to separate and divorce, Ted's fears about money have caused Yvonne to doubt herself and feel anxious.

Yvonne came to me because although she wanted to separate, she felt that she needed to understand the financial position so that she could feel confident about moving forward irrespective of what Ted thought. During our time together, Yvonne came to understand the family's financial position, what her income needed to be to move out of the family home (she knew that Ted would refuse), and how to rebuild her self-esteem.

Is it me?

Before we start this section, I'm going to invite you to grab a notebook and a pen. I'm a coach, and we coaches like to ask lots of questions! You can share your answers with me if you would like to at emma@emmaheptonstall.com, but for now, these answers are just for you.

To get the most out of this section, it would be great if you start by agreeing with yourself to be honest with your answers. Even if that's toe-curlingly embarrassing, or painful. No one else will know. When you're honest with yourself, you'll get clearer about where you're at and the steps you need to take.

Writing down your thoughts and feelings makes them more real. You are more likely to take action on something that's written down rather than just in your head. I'd love for this book to be thoroughly thumbed by the time you've finished with it. Notes in the margins, highlighted sections, whatever works for you. Make notes if it helps. Keep that notebook and pen close. Use it as a journal if you wish. It'll help you keep track of your progress when times get tough.

Ready?

Marriages rarely go wrong for no reason. The key to ending your marriage with clarity and confidence is understanding, and being sure of the reason. Now let me be clear, this isn't about blame – looking at whose fault it is. In truth, it takes two people to make a marriage work, and it takes two for it to fail. What matters is that you understand that and you understand the cause.

The reason for this is two-fold. Firstly, it may help you to figure out if your marriage is salvageable. Secondly, if you can 'see' that your marriage is definitely over, it will help you to move forward without looking back.

You need to be clear that you aren't running away from you. Is the source of unhappiness, frustration, misery and anger about the situation or about you? This might be the first time that you have considered this. So consider it now. You see, if the source of unhappiness is within you, it'll stay with you on divorce. You'll still be with you whether you move towns or stay in the same house. Except you won't have your husband any more. So how do you know if the issue is with you? Whether you're on your own or you begin a new relationship, some of the same issues will be there – the washing and ironing will need doing. You'll still be chasing your children – if you have them – about homework and screen time.

How are you, with you?

When you lead a busy life, it's easy to push thoughts and feelings down. Dealing with our emotions comes easier to some of us than others, and if you don't find it easy, it's likely that you haven't been making it a priority.

Do you like and love yourself? A strange question you might think, but it's key to working out how you are with yourself. What do you say to yourself when you look in the mirror? What do you say to yourself when something doesn't go according to plan? Are you kind and loving, or do you put yourself down?

Katie

Katie is in her 40s. She's been with her husband Will since her late teens. Katie feels confused. Katie feels that she's spent so long with Will that she's lost her identity. She is a wife and mother. Katie longs for that feeling of being outgoing and fun. She is anxious and scared that 'Katie' has disappeared.

Like Angela, Katie's husband belittled her and made her feel unloveable and small, even though Katie was the main carer for their three children – one of whom has complex needs.

Katie doubted herself. She doubted her decision to leave and whether that would make her a 'bad' mother, and also the impact upon Will, whom she cared about, and still does, deeply. Katie struggled with the fact that Will has unresolved childhood issues which led to unkind and abusive behaviour. But this led to Katie minimising the impact of his behaviour on her own self-esteem.

Katie and I worked together to look at 'Katie' as a wife and mother and also as a woman, a friend, a daughter and as a professional. We uncovered that Katie is a strong, rational, loving, caring woman with her own values, strengths and friendships. Katie began to see that she is deserving of the life she wants and that she isn't responsible for her husband.

Angela

Angela isn't proud of the fact that she is having an affair. It's not something that she ever thought she'd do, but her marriage is killing her spirit. Richard makes Angela feel alive. But what if she and Richard don't make it? What if both Angela and Richard are on the rebound? What then?

Working together, we uncovered Angela's core beliefs about herself. Funny, strong, kind, and loving. Not wasteful, pathetic and uneducated as her husband Michael repeatedly told her. Angela was able to see she didn't need Michael or Richard. The question was, which one of them, if either, did she want?

You see, you are always showing other people how to treat you. Even when you don't say it out loud. The way you hold yourself, the way you respond to others, gives clues about who you think you are and how you deserve to be treated.

When you don't feel good about you, it's more likely that you will be struggling in your relationship. It doesn't mean that the relationship is over. **It means that you need to do some work on you.**

 # Action Point

Have you heard of affirmations? Affirmations are a way to positively reinforce thoughts we have. Do you notice how you often talk to yourself and put yourself down? That's a way of repeatedly affirming something negative to yourself.

This exercise is the opposite of that. It may feel crazy and weird at first, but with practice, it works. Practice is key. Do this every day in front of the mirror. You can whisper it at first if that's easier but I want you to progress to saying the affirmations out loud, with feeling and with a smile on your face. Deal?

» Firstly, you need to create your affirmations. It's best to write these down and read them until you have them memorised.
» Affirmations are always a positive statement as if it has already happened. The more you tell your brain that these things are true, the quicker they'll become true for you.
» Choose five statements.

Examples include:

I am confident
I am worthy
I'm a great mother/friend/sister/daughter
I am happy
I am relaxed

Now, before you tell me you don't feel those things, I know. But you will if you put the work in and do the exercises.

» Stand in front of a mirror and, looking yourself in the eyes, say the affirmations out loud.
» Notice that you might feel 'silly' or uncomfortable — that's completely normal. Just push through it and keep going.

» Repeat your set of 5 affirmations 3 times.

» Repeat these every day.

You can do them before or after you brush your teeth morning or evening – both if you can. Whatever. Just do it. You can use the examples above or choose your own.

When your relationship is the cause of your low self-esteem

Sometimes the cause of your low self-esteem is your relationship. The way that your husband treats you and speaks to you. Perhaps before you met him you were a smart confident woman and you feel like that's all gone now. It's important that you begin to consider these issues before you call time on your marriage. If your self-esteem issues come from the relationship you have *with* your husband, leaving may be a serious option for you if he isn't willing to get support for his behaviour and the way the two of you interact with each other. See Section 2 on domestic abuse and Section 7 later in the book to consider the patterns in your relationship. Katie said, "A combination of fear, loss, grief and the need for familiarity and hedging bets means that staying in these patterns is a way of remaining in the relationship."

If, on the other hand, you know that your issues are with you, you always have the choice of dealing with them, rather than blaming your marriage and leaving.

Action Point

Let's look for a moment at Katie and Angela. Katie and Angela considered themselves to be smart, together women. But when it came to their marriage, they doubted themselves. Read their stories again and notice what comes up for you. Can you relate? Write down your thoughts and look at them in black and white. How does it feel; what thoughts come up for you?

Where is your marriage at?

At the time of reading this book, where is your marriage at? How long have you been thinking about leaving? When I started my business, I asked many divorced ladies how long they'd waited to leave their marriages before they actually left. The average was five years. Some ladies waited 15 years and others as long as 18 years. What's going through your mind, and how do you feel in your stomach when you read that? Can you relate? How do you feel in your relationship? How is the communication between you and your husband?

Action Point

» Write down how long you've been having these feelings.
» How do you feel in your relationship?
» How is the communication between you and your husband?
» Write a letter to your husband to tell him how you feel and what you want from him. Here's the thing, you don't have to send it. If it won't be received well, could place you in danger

of harm or will make things worse, DON'T send it. But write it – you'll find it a useful way of getting clarity. Burn it if you must once it's done. If you can give it to him, it may start a conversation to allow you to visit issues. Consider seeing a relationship counsellor (see **Relationship counselling** later in this section).

» Visit bit.ly/Howtobealadywholeavesbookresources and work through the exercise *7 Simple Steps*.

What do you really want?

Figuring out what you really want before you make decisions about your marriage will help you to make a smart decision. It may be a long time since you asked yourself that question. I'm not just talking here about whether you want to be married to your husband, I'm talking about the vision that you hold for yourself in your life. Being married is only part of that.

 *Action Point*

What's important to you?

Understanding what's important to you is the first step to moving forward. In my 7 Step Divorce System, I help my clients get clear about their values. It is a three-month programme I take clients through to get divorce ready. You can find out more about it at www.emmaheptonstall.com/divorce-coaching/7-step-divorce-system.

On a day-to-day basis, you probably don't consider what your values are because they are an intrinsic part of you. Unhappy?

I'd guess it's because one or more of your values aren't being met. Now some of the things that you value will 'have' value. Value in the financial sense. Your home, your car, perhaps a piece of jewellery or furniture. I'm not talking about those things. I'm talking about the things in your life that are important to you.

You may never have considered this before. That's okay because these things are so much part of us that we aren't consciously aware of them until someone asks. So, I'm asking!

 ## Action Point

Consider what's important to you about your health. Words like 'fitness', 'weight' and 'appearance' might come up for you. None of these might come up, but lots of other words might.

Write a list. Remember that this is your list. There are no 'right' and 'wrong' answers. There are only YOUR answers.

You can also work out your values by how you lead your life (or not). For example, if being physically fit is important to you, it's likely that you make it a priority in your life. You'll be going running, to exercise classes or the gym on a regular basis. When you're planning your day, it'll be one of the first things you schedule in, and not one of the last. If (for whatever reason) you're not able to keep up with your exercise routine, it's likely that you'll feel unhappy about it, maybe even a bit depressed. Why? Because a need in you isn't being met. With me so far? Great. I'm sure you can see where this is going ...

So. Let's look at what's important to you about your relationship. What words are coming up for you? Just like for your health, write them down. Visit bit.ly/Howtobealadywholeavesbookresources for a worksheet on values. It's important that you don't censor yourself right now. Just do it. Write whatever comes to mind. Remember, no right or wrong, there's just you and only you are going to see this (unless you choose to share it).

You might find this part of the exercise more challenging. It might bring up feelings of sadness, anger, frustration, loss, guilt to name but a few, and it might not. Either is the way it is for you. Just promise yourself that you'll do this openly and honestly.

As I said, if your values aren't met consistently over a long period of time, it's likely you'll be unhappy. Let go of your values for long enough, and it may be that you've lost touch with them.

Done your list?

Great.

How do you feel? How does it seem looking at that list? Before I do anything else with my clients, we dive deep to find out what's important to them. This information is gold dust. It's the beginning of finding out whether they should stay or go.

How many of your values are currently being met in your relationship? Take some time to consider this. You may know very quickly or you may need some time to process this.

The happiness question

The media often talks about 'happy' marriages as if there's some secret formula that we must all adhere to. In my professional experience, everyone's definition of a happy marriage is different. What is your idea of happiness and how close is your marriage to that? What are you willing to do to change things in your marriage? I say this because it's important to remember that you can't change your husband. Only he can do that – if he's willing and able.

Communication

If you aren't happy in your relationship, I'd guess that you and your husband are struggling with your communication? The thing about communication issues is that they rarely occur all of a sudden. Loss of communication usually occurs over a period of time, so insidiously that you may not have even noticed. It might be that just reading these words is helping you reflect and recognise that you and your husband aren't communicating. Communication is the cornerstone of any relationship. Without communication, there can be no intimacy. Without communication, there can only be 'I' not 'we'.

Loss of communication happens because you're busy or tired. It happens because you can't be bothered to disagree. It happens because your husband works late and after you have sorted out the children, eaten, and fallen onto the sofa to watch some TV, you fall asleep. Lack of communication is literally the silent killer of relationships.

Is our relationship a lost cause then?

If you were hoping that you would see some kind of flowchart in this book that would tell you whether or not you should leave your husband, I'm sorry to disappoint you. It really isn't as simple as that. If only it were?!

Whether your relationship is a lost cause or not is complicated. It really depends. It depends on you, on him, and on each of you being willing and open to addressing the issues in your relationship.

What are you willing to do? Now that you know what you want, are you willing to share it with your husband? Remember that men are not mind readers. They really don't get our subtle hints. Fact. If you want him to know something, you just have to come right out and say. He won't see it as the big deal you do. So if you don't tell him, he won't know.

 Action Point

What's stopping you from being open with your husband? Write down all the things that are stopping you. Even if you're not sure if something is stopping you write it down anyway.

Done that? Great!

Is it real? Now look back at all those things that you wrote down, and ask yourself if those reasons are real, or have you made them up in your head because it's scary and you're fearful of the response? Be honest. Go on, you can do this. You don't need to have a judgement about yourself; you are the way you are. But if you recognise that you're making reasons up in your head, it gives you the opportunity to do something different. If you want to continue making things up in your head, what is that telling you about your relationship?

What would happen if you did tell your husband what's going on for you? Write it down. Perhaps you're worried about his reaction? That's normal. But let me ask you this: how would it be if you just found the courage to tell him and accepted the consequences? In what ways would that clarity bring you closer to a decision? What if the response is positive? What then? If you've not been communicating for a while, can you really be sure of his reaction?

If you really aren't willing to communicate with your husband, what does that mean to you? Could the support of relationship counselling help? Are you willing to suggest and try it? Do you care enough to want to try? It's okay not to want to, you know. This is about tapping into what you really want; this is not about what you 'should' do. There are no 'shoulds' in this book. Perhaps you're realising and getting clear for the first time that you don't want to try any more.

This realisation may bring up many fears. Thoughts about what will happen, what you need to do, and how you'll cope. The children. Money. The dog. Oh My Goodness!

So if this is you, what should you do? The first thing that you should do is nothing. That's right. You read that right. Do nothing. Sit with your decision; just be. After all, what's the rush? Sitting with the decision can be uncomfortable particularly if you are the sort of lady who likes doing stuff. The sort of lady who likes making a decision and just doing it. Whoa girl, there's plenty of time. The more comfortable you get with the decision, the easier you'll find it to share it.

Sometimes, I help my clients figure out what to say and how to say it. Sometimes it's just an overview. Another of my clients liked to write down word for word what to say. She practised it, getting confident in her words so that when she delivered them, she could deliver them with confidence and clarity. If you want to tell your husband that you're leaving, tell him when you have that confidence and clarity. Not only will you believe you, he will also believe you. The more certainty you have with you, the less able he will be to undermine you.

 ## Action Point

Write down in detail, or in bullet point form, what you want to say to your husband. Remember that sharing your decision with him does not need to include justification or any specific details. Keep it short and sweet and always talk from 'I'. Talking from 'I' means that you cannot be wrong. For example, "I want to leave because I feel our marriage is over. I'm not in love with you any more." Talking from 'I' also avoids blame. Blame will not do anything for you at this point (or ever).

Practise whatever it is you're going to say in front of a mirror if it helps you. That might sound odd but if you're struggling with the confidence to say what you need to say, practising in front of the mirror whilst looking yourself in the eyes will help you develop that certainty and confidence in yourself. Say it like you mean it.

Relationship counselling

I don't do relationship counselling, but I'm a great advocate for it. Why? Because it works. Simple. Very few people get absolutely nothing from it. You see, to go to relationship counselling, you need to be willing. Both of you need to be willing. Which is good, right? If you're not willing, that says a lot about the state of the relationship and you probably need to go more than ever.

And it's always your choice.

If I needed to go to relationship counselling would I? Absolutely!

Have you tried relationship counselling? Many of my clients have already been to a relationship counsellor by the time they come to me, but not everyone has. That's okay. Relationship counselling is a safe and supportive place for you to share what you're thinking and feeling. A trained counsellor is there to help you express those feelings by asking you questions to help you open up and explore what's really going on for you.

Relationship counselling can be daunting. You might have seen a counsellor on your own before, and it would've been just you and them. A safe place just to say whatever you want, even about your husband. But in relationship counselling, your partner is there with you listening, observing and taking in your thoughts and feelings. The support of a relationship counsellor can be invaluable for helping you to share difficult emotions. You won't be on your own, and neither will your husband. It's also possible for you to attend relationship counselling on your own to talk through your thoughts with the counsellor. You might do this if your husband disengages.

Even if you or your husband aren't the greatest talkers, relationship counsellors use a variety of ways to support your communication to move forward. It really depends upon the two of you, what you want and what will work best.

You may use relationship counselling to talk about the issues that you are experiencing in your current relationship or those that are impacting you from the past. You may find doing this is beneficial even if you feel that your relationship is over because dealing with these issues now means it is less likely that you'll take them forward to a new relationship.

Listening and feeling heard

In relationship counselling you get the opportunity to listen, really listen. You probably think you do. We all like to think we listen. But when we are fed up, angry and emotional there can be a mismatch between what is said and what we hear. A relationship counsellor is trained to help you recognise the difference, and to really hear what is being said. This can make a massive difference to your relationship, and it may be the thing that saves it. Equally, it may be the thing that allows you to recognise that your relationship is definitely done.

Speaking your truth

Speaking the truth can be hard. When you care about somebody, even if you're no longer in love with them, hurting them is not on your agenda. So what do you do? You keep it all in. That's what causes some of the problems in relationships because unconsciously, that dissatisfaction, that unhappiness, that anger and frustration comes out in other small ways. You may pride yourself that there's no fighting in your relationship. You may boast to friends that "we never argue". Oh really? Well, you might never argue but that doesn't mean you're open, honest, getting on well together and truly happy in your relationship, does it? Relationship counselling is designed to get underneath what's really going on in your relationship so that you can be open and honest in a kind and supportive way.

How often do you attend relationship counselling?

This depends upon you and your partner. You might go every week for an hour for a set number of weeks, or you might go less frequently than that. One session may be enough to restart the communication in your relationship. For others, several sessions may be needed.

My relationship is over; what can I get out of a relationship counselling?

Going to relationship counselling doesn't necessarily mean that you've decided to stay in your relationship either. You may use relationship counselling as a venue for sharing with your husband that the relationship is over. You can decide to use relationship counselling as the place to explore the practicalities of the end of your relationship on a day-to-day basis. You might want to discuss how you are going to tell the children about your separation, what will happen with the family home in the immediate future, what arrangements there are for the children, and how you'll manage financially.

Angela

Before they began the divorce process, Angela and Michael returned to relationship counselling. Angela was convinced that she wanted to divorce. She was tired and fed up with the way Michael spoke to her, criticising her for her kitchen skills and the way she parented their child. During our first coaching session, Angela and I worked on her self-esteem. It had been a lightbulb moment for her – she recognised that she wanted and deserved to be treated better.

When Angela first told Michael that she wanted to divorce, he asked her to try relationship counselling again. Angela was reluctant at first, because she saw it as yet another way of Michael resisting the reality of their situation. Angela felt frustrated as she was ready to move forward.

Angela and I explored how going to relationship counselling might support her and Michael to accept that the relationship was over and how they could both move forward.

Angela attended a number of relationship counselling sessions in accordance with Michael's wishes but she did not change her mind about divorce. For Angela, relationship counselling was useful in that she felt supported to be open and honest with Michael in an environment where Michael was supported to hear what Angela was saying.

How much does relationship counselling cost?

The cost of relationship counselling varies across the country as each counselling service is independent even though they may be part of a larger network such as Relate. If you find relationship counselling with a charitable organisation you can expect there to be a waiting list. But investing in relationship counselling will give both of you clarity which you may find to be priceless.

So you'd recommend it then Emma?

Yes! Yes I would and I do! You'll learn a lot about yourself and how you communicate. You'll learn more about who you really are and also learn more about your husband too. The key to a great marriage is communication. I also believe it's the key to a great divorce. So if you're both willing, give it a go. You'll be glad you did, whatever the outcome.

The decision

I'm not a lady who leaves, so what next?

So you decided that you're not going to be a lady who leaves: well done! How does it feel to have made that decision? Good I hope! Like I said earlier, I'm a great believer in marriage and the fact that you want to continue to explore working on your marriage is fantastic.

Make a list of the things that you want to talk to your husband about. Figure out what it is you're willing to ask for and what you are willing to give. Yes, give. Giving is an important part of receiving; it's part of the relationship process. Visit my website at bit.ly/Howtobealadywholeavesbookresources to download resources and contact information to support you to get your relationship back on track. Know also that you can revisit this section any time you need to check in with yourself. Ensure that you continue to ask for what you want and need, and that you get your needs met. Keep the lines of communication open!

I am a lady who is going to leave

If, having worked through this section, you decide that for the moment at least, you're going to be a lady who leaves, the rest of this book is for you. The following sections will deal with the divorce law of England and Wales, the application process, timescales and everything that you need to consider. We will also look at how family mediation can help you, how to deal with your finances, how to resolve arrangements regarding your children and how to move on after the divorce process.

Section 2

Domestic abuse
– Nina Farr

Introducing Nina Farr

This book is not designed for ladies who are experiencing domestic abuse in their marriage. But it would be remiss of me not to include a section on it in this book, so Nina Farr, expert parenting coach, will guide you through. Over to you Nina.

I'm Nina Farr, and I'm a leadership coach who specialises in working with women who are parenting alone. Many of my clients have experienced relationships that fall somewhere on the spectrum of 'high-conflict' separations or divorces. I also work with women who have been the victim of domestic violence or abuse.

Recognising abusive relationships

Recognising when you are (or have been) in an abusive relationship is not always as simple as it sounds. Abuse forms a pattern of behaviours over a long period of time. Often the victim becomes so used to the abuse that they no longer recognise that it is outside of the normal, healthy range of relationships. If you are not sure whether your relationship is normal, I'd like to share some specialist information here that will help you to take stock of what's happening at home. I hope after reading this section you will understand the difference between a state of high conflict (which may make you feel victimised) and being a victim of domestic abuse.

It's an unfortunate fact that separations can bring out the worst in people. When people are in pain, it's common for them to lash out. Both men and women are vulnerable to feelings of rage, hurt, abandonment and pain that can sometimes trigger unacceptable behaviour on either side. This is what I would describe as a 'high-conflict' separation experience. Sometimes this kind of conflict arises close to or after the separation; it may not have been a pattern throughout the relationship up to that point. Sometimes the pattern of conflict is well established and has contributed to a couple deciding to separate.

If one or both of you are in a state of heightened emotion, feeling trapped, frightened or angered by a separation that appears out of their control, communication can deteriorate rapidly. If you feel very panicky or anxious about leaving it is hard to keep communication around your divorce plans calm. If you find yourself becoming unable to see, speak to, or even talk about your ex (or they about you) without feeling angry or very upset, then you're experiencing a high-conflict separation.

This level of stress will inhibit progress in your divorce, negatively impact your children, and can cost a lot of money and time in lawyers' bills. It is usually characterised by both parties treating their feelings as if they were facts. For example, 'I feel out of control' so this must mean my ex is controlling the divorce process. When both parties feel out of control, it's easy to see how communication breaks down. As hard as it may seem, separating feelings from facts is the pathway to a constructive divorce for high-conflict couples.

Conflict is draining, overwhelming and destructive. It is rarely dangerous though. In many cases, a good family mediator can help support warring separating couples to communicate better, and Emma has some great suggestions later in this book about how to access this if you think it would help in your case.

However, domestic violence or abuse is not just tempers flaring into short-term conflict. Attempting to negotiate with or appease your abuser as you try to leave them can indeed be dangerous. For this reason, mediation with your abusive husband is not usually appropriate (the mediator will assess your suitability at your Mediation Information and Assessment Meeting (MIAM)).

What is domestic abuse?[1]

The cross-government definition of domestic violence and abuse is: "Any incident of controlling, coercive, threatening behaviour, violence or abuse between those aged 16 or over who are, or have been, intimate partners or family members regardless of gender or sexuality. The abuse can encompass, but is not limited to: psychological, physical, sexual, financial and emotional."

Controlling behaviour is a range of acts designed to make a person subordinate and/or dependent by isolating them from sources of support, exploiting their resources and capacities for personal gain, depriving them of the means needed for independence, resistance and escape, and regulating their everyday behaviour.

Coercive behaviour is an act or pattern of acts of assaults, threats, humiliation and intimidation or other abuse that is used to harm, punish or frighten their victim.

Family members are defined as mother, father, son, daughter, brother, sister, and grandparents, whether directly related, in-laws or stepfamily.

Domestic abuse occurs across society, regardless of age, gender, race, sexuality, wealth, and geography.

---

1   Information in this section taken from www.gov.uk under OGL http://www.nationalar-chives.gov.uk/doc/open-government-licence/version/1/open-government-licence.htm

How do I know if my relationship is abusive?

Reading this definition can be very upsetting the first time if you recognise your own situation in it. If you feel upset now, take some time away from the book to consider what you have just read. Which part of the statement above has caused you to feel upset? Which parts do you recognise or relate to? To what extent do you feel the statement applies to you?

It may be helpful to speak to someone about what you are experiencing. If you do not have a supportive friend or family member to turn to, you can call the 24 hour National Domestic Violence Freephone Helpline on 08002000247. The lines are staffed by fully trained, sympathetic volunteers and staff who can listen, comfort and advise you in person. You may find it helps to describe your experiences to someone to help gain clarity around what is happening to you right now.

However, for many women in controlling relationships this statement does not trigger a complete awareness or understanding of their abuse. Coercive control unfolds over a long period of time. Depending how long you have been in a controlling relationship you may have come to accept behaviour designed to control you as normal. This skewed sense of what a relationship should be like has kept many of my clients in abusive relationships long after an objective outsider might suggest they leave.

It is common for abused women who have not been physically attacked to not realise they are being abused. If your partner has not hit you, this does not automatically mean you are not a victim of domestic abuse. Sadly, violence is not the only kind of abuse that you may have experienced. Even if your partner has never been physically violent, you may still be a victim of domestic abuse. Abuse occurs in a pattern, and can take many forms:

Source :
http://www.theduluthmodel.org/wp-content/uploads/2017/03/PowerandControl.pdf
Used with kind permission of www.theduluthmodel.org

The Power and Control Wheel graphic was created in Minnesota, in 1982,out of the experience of women who were victims of domestic violence and abuse. As such it represents the lived experience of women who live with a man who is violent towards them. It is characterised by the pattern of actions that an individual uses to intentionally control or dominate his intimate partner. This is why the words 'power and control' are in the centre of the wheel. A perpetrator of domestic violence or abuse systematically uses threats, intimidation or coercion to instill fear in his partner. These behaviours are the spokes of the wheel.

This wheel shows some of the many ways your partner may be exerting control over your life right now. You can see from this wheel that not all of the ways you can be abused are easy to pinpoint by yourself. If your husband is intimidating or threatening, but also blames you and minimises his behaviour, you are likely to feel both anxious and confused. You may find it hard to describe what is happening or doubt your own perception of reality. In the absence of being hit, raped or otherwise assaulted, it's easy to question if you are even being abused at all.

If you think your partner may be controlling you, it may help to ask yourself these questions. It may be helpful to write down your answers, but if you are afraid that they may be found by your partner afterwards take care to keep them in a private place or destroy them when you are finished working on this section.

Ask yourself:

» Am I being limited in my choices and freedoms in this relationship?
» Do I make excuses for his actions, blaming myself when things go wrong?
» Does he seem to forget, minimise or deny when things go wrong, shifting the responsibility onto me?

» Am I ever afraid, anxious or overly-aware that my actions may trigger a negative reaction in my husband?
» Has my husband ever directly frightened, intimidated or hurt me when we disagree?

Can you see your husband's behaviour in this pattern?

Cycle of Abuse

1 Tensions Building
Tensions increase, breakdown of communication, victim becomes fearful and feels the need to placate the abuser

4 Calm
Incident is "forgotten", no abuse is taking place. The "honeymoon" phase

2 Incident
Verbal, emotional & physical abuse. Anger, blaming, arguing. Threats. Intimidation.

3 Reconciliation
Abuser apologizes, gives excuses, blames the victim, denies the abuse occured, or says that it wasn't as bad as the victim claims

Source :
www.wikipedia.org/wiki/Cycle_of_abuse

Before we hear more from Nina, I'd like you to consider the next action point.

Action Point

Read Katie's story:

Katie

Katie's experience of domestic abuse is very common. In our early months working together, Katie resisted any suggestion that her relationship with her husband was abusive. Sometimes Katie wanted to talk to me because of an incident that occurred between her and her husband. On such occasions, Katie would be openly vulnerable, tearful and both angry and distraught. She would share the verbal abuse she experienced from her husband without censoring, minimising or defending his behaviour. On other occasions, Katie would want to talk more practically about divorce. On these occasions, Katie would seek to explain away, justify and worry about her husband's ability to cope without her.

Katie was very keen to use family mediation. Although asset rich, Katie and Will were cash poor and so Katie was keen to keep the legal costs down. Katie also wanted to support her husband by using mediation as a way of talking through their financial matters and their childcare arrangements in a calm and supportive environment.

When Katie initially left the family home, she decided it would be best for the children if they postponed divorce until they were more settled into the routine of having two homes. For a period, Katie and Will's relationship appeared to improve. It didn't last. Will began turning up at Katie's house and verbally abusing her in front of the children, reducing her to tears. As Katie began to share more of the history of her husband's behaviour, she began to accept that her husband's behaviour was abusive. It's something that Katie is still struggling to accept. Family mediation was not appropriate for her.

Can you relate to the way in which Katie oscillated between denial and acceptance of her husband's behaviour? How does that show up in the way that you cope in your own relationship? Write about this in your journal or notebook. How does it feel? Make some notes before we pick up with Nina again …

It may not be something as obvious as physical or sexual violence. You may recognise this pattern playing out in many ways, resulting in a range of outcomes from agreeing to wear clothes he prefers, through to giving up on being granted access to money, food or other resources he deems unnecessary. You may feel disempowered around how you parent, if or where you work, what you wear, eat, buy or if/how you travel. This pattern is usually very repetitive. It strips away another little layer of the abused partner's identity, independence and resilience.

Abusers are in control of themselves when they abuse. Unlike the high-conflict, emotionally overwhelmed person who is lashing out indiscriminately, abusers have a pattern of behaviour directed at the person they intend to control. This may be you, your children, or other vulnerable people they are in close contact with.

If your husband is lashing out at a time of high emotional stress – for example, because one of you has raised the subject of divorce – you might find it hard to tell whether he is victimising you or simply unable to cope with his own negative feelings. To help you decide if your husband is overwhelmed (and lashing out, in a high-conflict style) or abusive, ask yourself these questions:

1. Is he violent or threatening with his boss, friends or co-workers?

In the majority of cases, abusers are not violent with those they hope to be seen favourably by, or who are in a position of dominance over them.

2. Is he able to compose himself or put on a 'public face' when other people are close by?

Abusers can shift between apparent rage or contempt towards you, into a positive and friendly aspect in front of other people. You may feel bewildered, confused, and as if you are walking on eggshells because you do not know which 'face' you will be met by at any given time. Other people have no idea that your abuser is capable of behaving this way, further isolating you.

3. Does he isolate you from your friends, family or co-workers?

An abusive relationship relies upon the victim having little or no feedback about what they are experiencing. By reducing your contact with people who care about you, your abuser is able to keep you in a state of confusion and dependency that perpetuates their control over you.

4. If he uses physical violence, does he choose where to cause injuries, aiming for places where other people cannot see them?

For example, squeezing your upper arms to the point of bruising, or striking you on the torso or legs instead?

If you husband is physically hurting you or your children in any way, you are experiencing domestic violence. You may have formed a habit of excusing his behaviour, believing that if he doesn't 'hit' you, but bruises you in ways he claims are accidental, that this is your fault. It is never your fault when your partner is physically or emotionally harming you on purpose.

Becoming able to recognise that you are being abused is a painful and frightening realisation for many women. For many, the actions of their abusive partner have developed over years with the effect of boiling a frog – you don't know you are in hot water until it's too late to jump to safety!

Please trust me that you are neither alone, trapped, nor stupid if you have arrived in this place. There is help available to you and you can escape. Keep reading this section to find out what you can do to keep yourself and your children safe as you plan your next steps.

Physical violence is almost always one of the last forms of abuse to occur. Most wives and children of violent men have experienced coercive control and psychological and emotional abuse before they are physically abused. This can be both helpful in recognising that abuse is taking place before it descends into physical violence, and unhelpful, because the emotional and psychological abuse is so pervasive. If you are experiencing a relationship that has stripped away your confidence or ability to take charge of your next steps you will need some extra support.

How does experiencing domestic violence and abuse change the divorce process?

First and foremost: your priority is to stay safe.

The most dangerous point in an abusive relationship is often when the abused partner attempts to leave. Realising that their control is about to end can tip abusive partners into their worst and most dangerous behaviour. It is a fact that the peak of violent or otherwise abusive behaviour usually occurs at or around the point of separation.

I am not sharing this to scare you, although it may be frightening to think about – it is important to know that things may indeed get worse before they get better, in order to prepare yourself for being a lady who leaves an abusive relationship.

With your safety and that of any children you share being your priority, it is important to stay calm while you make your plan to leave. This is called making a safety plan. I will give you some pointers here about things to consider, but it is almost always better, if you can, to make this plan with another person. Safeguarding is everyone's responsibility and there are many people who can and will help you to leave. Suggestions are listed at the end of this section.

The most skilled people to ask for help are domestic abuse services. When you approach a professional domestic abuse agency they will often ask for your permission to go through a questionnaire. These questions help them to understand what your current risk is and how they can best keep you safe.

Safety planning before you leave

Documents: Collect your essential documents before you consider having a conversation about leaving with your husband. These should include:

» yours and your children's passports, birth certificates or other forms of identity
» bank statements or copies of bank statements for any personal or shared accounts if you can access these
» documentary evidence of other assets if you have any
» copies of any legal agreements you may already have (injunctions, child arrangements orders for example)

Belongings: Keep a small bag packed with clothes for yourself and your children, and always carry some cash in case you need to leave in a hurry.

» Store personal items in your car or at a friend's house who knows you may need to arrive at short notice.
» Keep your phone with you at all times, or purchase a PAYG phone (with credit topped up!) to keep in your safety bag.
» Before you leave, ensure you have the children's special items with you if possible (bedtime toys, special photographs).
» Pack anything that may be used as a bargaining chip to get you to come home again if this is unlikely to be safe: sentimental or valuable jewellery, family photos etc.

Children: Do not plan to leave without telling someone you and any children you have are at risk.

» Inform their school or childcare provider that you are leaving an abusive relationship and let them know you will be collecting them from school or care going forwards. They may not be able to prevent your husband from collecting the children but may be able to inform you if this happens without your consent.

» Take your children with you when you leave. If you do not, it may become difficult or impossible for them to live with you after the event.

You can find a detailed safety plan listed on Women's Aid here www.womensaid.org.uk/the-survivors-handbook/making-a-safety-plan.

Going forward towards a divorce, after you have left

The divorce process itself may be affected in many practical ways by abuse, not all of which I can detail here. The first thing to prepare yourself for is the fact that even if your relationship ends, this may not mean your abuser stops abusing you. The divorce process can open you up to new channels of abuse if you are unsupported. I cannot advise you strongly enough: if you believe you are being abused, please reach out for real world support from a professional agency or legal professional. You will be eligible for legal aid (financial assistance to pay for your legal bills) only if you can provide evidence that you or your children are at risk from your husband, and that you are unable to pay for your own legal costs.

You or your children must have been victims of domestic abuse or violence, or financial control (being prevented from accessing a shared bank account for example), to qualify for legal aid. It is not enough to simply say you have been abused after you leave, to access legal aid. You will need to provide evidence. In almost all cases, it is easier to gather some of this evidence before you leave. Reporting what you are experiencing to a professional will mean there is a record of what is happening in your home, which you may later need to rely upon in court.

You can ask for evidence from:

» the courts
» the police
» a multi-agency risk assessment conference (MARAC)
» social services
» a health professional, e.g. a doctor, nurse, midwife, psychologist or health visitor
» a refuge manager
» a domestic violence support service
» your bank, e.g. credit card accounts, loan documents and statements
» your employer, or education or training provider
» the provider of any benefits you've received

A particularly emotionally difficult aspect of divorcing your abusive husband arises when you share children. In practical terms, you may not be able to stay together in the family home prior to deciding how to split any shared assets. It may be that something happens (a crisis event such as being attacked) meaning you must leave the family home yourself. If you do not leave the family home but it is not safe for your husband to retain access, you may need to apply for an occupation order (to keep a violent partner away from the shared home) or a non-molestation order (to keep him away from you). You will need specialist legal advice in this case, and I recommend finding a lawyer who is experienced in working with domestic violence and abuse. A domestic violence service will be able to give you a local recommendation.

In addition to the problems you may face keeping you and your children safe, you may not have access to financial information. This could disadvantage you in the divorce process as the legal process unfolds. If there are no records of your abuse, your husband may deny it has taken place at all. This is why it is so vital to include professionals in your safety plan as soon as possible. As frightening as it is to share what is happening to you now, it is the single most protective factor you can create for yourself and your family as you move forward.

If you are in immediate danger, none of these potential pitfalls, financial or emotional, are as important as you staying safe. Always choose leaving over procrastinating if your instincts are telling you to leave. In the worst case scenario, you leave with nothing but your life. Seven women a month are still killed by a former or current partner in England and Wales, so if in doubt, leave immediately.

However, if you are not at risk of physical harm today, try as far as is possible to prepare for what comes next calmly, purposefully and with hope. Gather support before you decide to leave – be that a connection with an IDVA (Independent Domestic Violence Advisor), through a support service, a place to stay with friends, some money that you can access by yourself, or specialist legal advice. The more prepared you are, the easier the transition to divorced life will be.

You can find help and support from:

» your GP, who can keep records of any injuries or emotional distress caused by your abuse (remember this may be vital evidence in the future if you need to prove in court that your ex is abusive)
» your child's school, health visitor, or local children's centre can put in practical steps to look after you and your children's wellbeing
» your midwife or baby clinic can signpost you to specialist support, and are usually very swift responders to families in need
» your local domestic abuse support service (Google them at your local library if you do not feel safe doing so at home)
» Women's Aid
» the National Domestic Violence Helpline (as above)

What will happen to my children if I leave their abusive father?

Ultimately, they will have a happier, healthier, more loving and enjoyable life. Hold this in mind if you find yourself wavering when the going gets tough. Divorce is never as harmful to children as growing up in an abusive home would be.

In addition to this, they will of course have to navigate a very difficult transition, just like you. Their father will likely be very angry about your decision to leave. In many cases, abusive fathers attempt to use contact with their children as a way to exert continued control over you, their mother, after a split. A child arrangements order will be granted as part of your divorce if you cannot come to an agreement about contact, residence or the religious/practical aspects of your children's upbringing after separation. As part of your child arrangements order you will specify the place your children are ordinarily resident (this used to be a separate residence order). Their residency is important to define, as it gives you the authority to ask for them to be returned to you by the police if necessary if your husband refuses to return them home after contact.

If your husband is violent or otherwise dangerous, your children may need to change their school or move house. Get help to decide if it is safer for you to leave the area where your abusive husband resides. This is a choice that can have financial consequences in the long term, which makes it feel very frightening to consider before you leave. Legal and professional support services are there to help you make this decision based on the facts, as well as how you feel. Gather these resources around you. You do not need to make such big decisions alone.

Know that there is no material comfort that can make up for experiencing a lifetime of abuse. Your children gain the most security and stability from their relationship with you, their non-abusive parent. Focus on what you will have more of, not what you will have less of, when you leave. You will have more freedom, more love, more opportunity for joy. Material things can be replaced, but a childhood filled with safety and love cannot.

Do not be afraid of pursuing residency, or strict boundaries around time spent with their father. If you are their main carer, family law in England and Wales favours the status quo, so their father cannot simply decide they will stay with him (even if he says or threatens that you will not be able to see them if you leave). Be prepared that he may attempt to discredit you, or may undermine your parenting to gain the upper hand. The best protection you have is to be honest with a professional about what has happened up until now, and to work with official agencies who can help you to record and evidence the impact of his actions on your children going forward. If you leave, take your children with you unless they or you are physically at risk in that moment. If you have to leave them, go directly to the police. Who your children reside with when you split will have considerable weight as time goes on.

HELP: I'm panicking now and I don't know what to do next

It all sounds very overwhelming I know, and at this point you might only be reading this book to decide if you want to leave! The realities of navigating a divorce with an abusive husband are as varied as the relationships that have led to that point. At a very basic level, the divorce process will remain much the same. However, the more you plan ahead for support, ask for help, and **build up a network of supportive professionals**, friends and family around you and your children, the easier this journey will be.

What will happen to my financial security if I leave my abusive partner?

It is impossible for me to know what your financial position may be while writing this section. While it would be comforting to offer a blanket answer here, the truth is, I don't know. Just like any other divorce, the financial settlement will depend largely on how the finances have been managed up until now. Have there been investments, or debts? In whose names have these decisions been made?

You may find that you are comfortably supported in your divorce, or you may not be. Working with your lawyer and a good counsellor who can help you to process the information as it comes out is the best protection you can give yourself.

If you are leaving without children, the long-term financial impact of your relationship will be revealed over time. Whatever the outcome, be aware that no amount of money would have soothed the hurt you have experienced through abuse. As you begin your healing journey, coming to terms with the many ways you have been let down will take time. If financial abuse has been part of that experience allow yourself to grieve for lost opportunities as fully as you grieve other aspects of your abuse. Do not let fear of poverty keep you stuck in a place of emotional poverty.

If you are leaving with children and find yourself financially unable to support or house them, you will not be left on the streets. Domestic abuse is a priority category for housing support. Many lone parent benefits are also expedited in the event that you find yourself suddenly alone with care of the children and no income. You may need to learn to budget very quickly and on a different scale to what you are used to now, but don't worry – you are capable, you can learn, and in time, your ability to step into leadership of your family and out of the shadow of your husband will empower you all.

Where can I find specialist support for myself and my children before I leave?

It can be hard to reach out and talk to people about what you're going through, I know. When you're used to keeping things secret, or minimising what's been happening at home, the thought of a conversation with someone about it can feel very frightening. If you're scared to tell someone about your abuse know that you are not alone in feeling like this, but it's not your secret to keep. The thought of telling someone what has happened and what you are afraid of is often much more scary than the reality.

If you are able to have this conversation with someone in person, you will be able to access support much more easily (and less easily traced) than simply by looking online for advice. Although domestic violence and abuse agencies should all have a 'cover your tracks' button on their websites (always look for this and click it before you leave a site – it will wipe the browser history so your husband cannot see what you've been researching), looking for information online can still be time consuming, and may not link you into real world services very fast.

When you reach out, talk to a professional with safeguarding training and responsibilities. This means someone who is in a position of authority or in a caring role – perhaps your child's school has a parent liaison or support worker. Your GP, health visitor or midwife are all great first ports of call. People in these roles should have been given training in recognising abuse, and know how to respond when someone shares information with them. They will have a legal duty to share what you tell them in order to keep you safe.

If you tell a friend or family member, be aware that they may give you advice that is not as helpful, sensitive or practical as a professional can. People who love us mean well, but often are not equipped to respond to a disclosure about domestic abuse. All their own preconceptions, concerns or questions will influence how they react. Don't take it personally if you share your experiences with someone who reacts badly. They are doing the best they can, as are you. A professional should be able to put you in touch with local services and help you make a risk assessment on your current situation – a friend or family member rarely knows how to do this with you.

Of course, if you have trusted friends or family who you feel you can tell as well, do share your situation with them. Open yourself up to emotional support as well as practical help. But be careful to choose only those who you trust not to talk to your husband as well. It can be difficult to know who this may be before you leave, so in the period before you leave, while you are planning how to do so safely, it is much better to rely on only a few very close people or professionals who can help you escape.

You can also try calling Women's Aid or the National Domestic Violence Helpline for supportive advice.

Thinking ahead: preparing to parent alone, or live alone, after abuse

Hold in your mind a vision of the life you are moving towards. I advise my clients to 'stretch their timeline' when thinking of the future. Remember that most people vastly overestimate what they can achieve in a year, and vastly underestimate what can change in 5–10 years. Life as a divorcée will look, feel and be very different to how life is today. Allow yourself the luxury of imagining how much better it has the potential to be long term.

When you powerfully connect with why you are leaving – to achieve a level of freedom, personal power, happiness and pride in yourself for example – the how will begin to unfold. This is the secret weapon in your divorce journey. Remembering that no matter what the obstacles are today, the opportunities tomorrow are worth it.

Know that your infinite power and potential is limited more profoundly not by your ex, but by yourself. When you give yourself permission to act with authority and purpose, you will indeed discover it within yourself.

You can find me at www.ninafarr.com or on Facebook at www.facebook.com/visionpurposepassion or on Twitter @LoneParentCoach. Please join my community of powerful lone parents, accessible through Facebook: www.facebook.com/groups/988831721231911/

How can I work with you if I leave my husband?

I offer a limited number of fully funded places on my 10-week 'Family Vision' course. This is a unique, extensively researched and tested leadership development programme for mothers who have experienced domestic violence or abuse in their relationships.

If you are unable to attend this programme in person but want to be part of a community of mothers parenting alone after abuse I also offer regular, small virtual coaching circles accessible via conference call from the comfort of your own home. You can find out more by joining my Facebook community or looking me up online.

If you are ready to take a leap into loving life after divorce, you can also join me on a transformational year of self-discovery, as part of my incredible mastermind groups for lone mothers, available in beautiful locations nationwide. This 10-month journey into powerful leadership of your family is crafted especially for women like you to unlock their best lives yet after divorce.

Section 3
Understanding the divorce process

Go to a lawyer when you're lost, confused, hurt and lacking in confidence, and the divorce process will seem like a complex nightmare. I understand. This section is designed to give you an overview of the divorce process so that by the time you visit a lawyer, the concepts and terms they share with you will already be familiar.

This book is all about the legal process of divorce in England and Wales. Will it support you in your jurisdiction? I don't know. You will need to check that out separately. If you live in England or Wales, or have the ability to divorce under the English law, this section is designed to support you in understanding the process. If you find it too much to digest in one go, take it step by step and re-read it. You can also check out the 'Understanding Divorce' action pack from my website. These cards will walk you through step by step everything that you need to know about the divorce and separation process, over a manageable 30-day period.

Who is entitled to divorce under English law?

Firstly, you must have been married for at least 12 months, and your marriage must have broken down irretrievably. You must also be resident or domiciled in England or Wales.

Domicile

The concept of domicile in family law is not the same as domicile for tax purposes. Domicile under family law means where you were born – your 'home'. But it is possible to change this. It is said that 'home is where the heart is' and this is particularly true in relation to family law. If England is your 'home' but you are living abroad, for example, you or your husband work in another country, but you still consider England to be home, then you are domiciled in England. You may therefore choose to divorce under English law. The rules around domiciliary are complex and should you be concerned whether they apply to you, you should seek specialist legal advice, but in essence, the domiciliary test is one of intention. For example, if you or your husband are on a contractual position abroad, you still own property in England, and you intend to return here in the future, you would be considered domiciled in England.

Habitually resident

If you are not domiciled in England or Wales, you may be able to apply for divorce under English law if you are habitually resident here. Habitually resident is not the same as being domiciled and the two should not be confused. Habitually resident means where you actually live, irrespective of your nationality, or where you were married. For divorce purposes, you must have been habitually resident in England or Wales for at least a year prior to your application for divorce. The habitually resident test is that you are physically present on a voluntary basis for a settled purpose with the intention to remain for a 'significant period' of time.

Can I get a divorce in another country?

Yes, it is possible. Sometimes the divorce process in another country may be more favourable for one spouse. This means that if there is a dispute about jurisdiction (where your divorce will take place from a legal point of view) from the start, you should seek specialist legal advice. Bear in mind that there can be substantially different processes in other countries. You will need to consider resolving your financial affairs in a way that is beneficial to you, so please consider this when choosing your jurisdiction.

If you were married in England or Wales and you have both lived here all your lives, the domiciliary and habitually resident test will not be an issue.

Criteria for applying for a divorce under English law:

» Both you and your spouse are habitually resident in England or Wales.
» Your spouse is habitually resident in England or Wales (you may live elsewhere).
» You and your spouse were last habitually resident in England or Wales and one of you still is.

» You are habitually resident in England or Wales and have been here for 12 months prior to application.
» You are domiciled and residing here for at least six months before issue.
» You and your husband are both domiciled in England and Wales (irrespective of where you live now).

Grounds for divorce

Did you know that there is only one ground for divorce in England and Wales? This is that your marriage has broken down irretrievably. This means that you are no longer willing or able to live with each other. Under English law, you show that your marriage has irretrievably broken down by proving one of five facts:

Adultery

If you are to be the petitioner (we look at this later) this must be your husband's adultery with a member of the opposite sex. You cannot apply for divorce on the grounds of your own adultery. If you wish to rely on adultery, you must cite it in your petition within six months of you finding out that your husband has been unfaithful. If more than six months have elapsed after you found out about it, you cannot rely on this ground. However, you can use the fact that he is in a relationship with someone else as an example of 'unreasonable behaviour' at any stage. His adultery may occur after you have physically separated (whether or not you still live together in the family home).

Unreasonable behaviour

This must be his unreasonable behaviour. There is no definition of unreasonable behaviour, but you must show that it is intolerable for you to continue to live with your husband. Some examples may include name-calling, financial abuse, excessive drinking, withholding sexual intercourse and bullying. It can also be his adultery – because he is in a relationship with another person. You do not need to find extreme examples (even though they exist), and often using these will complicate matters, so avoid using these if possible. There is a balance to be had between proving sufficient evidence and inflaming the situation for yourself.

Two years' separation with consent

You may apply for divorce on the grounds that you and your husband have been separated for at least two years preceding the application and both of you agree to the divorce. You may be separated whilst living in the same house. This is common. You are considered to be separated if you no longer share a bedroom, are no longer sexually intimate with each other and you're no longer cooking and cleaning or behaving in any way as if you are partners in a relationship.

Five years' separation

Perhaps you and your husband have been separated for five years or longer. It might be that you've just never got round to getting a divorce, it didn't feel right or he didn't want to. If you and your husband have been separated for five years preceding application, you do not need his consent to the divorce. It's wise, however, if you can, to discuss this with him and seek his opinion so that you are aware of what may happen next.

Desertion

Desertion is a ground rarely relied on today. You must prove that desertion occurred two years prior to the application for divorce, and that your husband intended to desert you. You might consider using this ground if your husband cannot be found but you don't believe him to be dead. If you and your husband accept the marriage is over, there are easier ways to ask for a divorce.

Which of the five facts should I choose?

It really depends. If you (for whatever reason) feel that you do not want to wait two or even five years, and you want an immediate divorce, the only options available to you are adultery or unreasonable behaviour. Remember that if you have known about your husband's adultery for more than six months you will be precluded from using this fact.

Both men and women often get very upset when being divorced on the fact of adultery because of the stigma and shame that still exists in society. It's important to remember that the court does not sit in judgement on anyone in respect of the five facts. Whichever of the five facts you choose to rely on, it will not have any bearing on your financial settlement.

It may be tempting when divorcing on the fact of adultery to name your husband's lover as a co-respondent to the divorce. You will be asked on the form if you wish to do this. Think twice. Pride, anger and frustration may lead you to want to do this but naming a co-respondent may delay your divorce and it's likely to inflame the situation. This will increase your costs. It is not legally necessary to name them, and it will have no bearing on the financial settlement or order that's made by the court.

Action Point

» Why do I want to name the other person?
» What will it achieve?
» How else can I deal with my emotions around this?
» What are the possible wider consequences of naming the other person?

By far the most common fact relied on in divorce is unreasonable behaviour. If you do decide to use unreasonable behaviour, remember that the court is only interested in determining whether the legal test has been met. As I said, the court does not sit in judgement on either of you, nor are they in the business of preventing people who want to divorce from doing so.

Angela

Angela, whose husband Michael often put her down and belittled her, just wanted to get divorced. She understood that it didn't matter whether she divorced him or he divorced her. During their discussions in relationship counselling, Angela offered to let Michael divorce her for her unreasonable behaviour if that would make him feel better. Initially, Michael agreed. Angela supported Michael and drew up the facts for their divorce, however, Michael dragged his feet and did not engage with that process. Therefore, Angela decided to divorce Michael.

This helped Angela move the divorce process forward. She did however help Michael complete the acknowledgement of service and to respond to the divorce petition when it arrived.

Katie

Katie was clear from the beginning that she wanted to divorce Will. Katie felt that by divorcing Will, like Angela, the process would move forward on her terms. Katie had many facts upon which she could divorce Will. Will had been verbally, emotionally and sadly physically abusive throughout their marriage. This had been discussed many times during their relationship counselling sessions. Will experienced what their therapist called 'toxic shame' and struggled to accept the abusive nature of his behaviour, choosing to minimise its impact and blame Katie.

When it came to the divorce petition, however, in order to progress matters Katie and I discussed how best to proceed by ensuring the divorce papers included enough detail of Will's unreasonable behaviour, in order that the legal test would be met, but not so much truth that Will would experience more toxic shame which would likely de-rail the divorce, adding both cost and unnecessary stress to Katie, Will and the children.

Action Point

- » Consider the ways in which your husband's behaviour is unreasonable.
- » Write down examples, dates where possible: a handful will do.
- » Consider how your husband may react when he receives the petition.
- » Is it likely he may agree, or is it likely he will be angry?

Even though I left, can he divorce me?

Yes! Sometimes my clients will agree to let their husbands divorce them for their unreasonable behaviour, even though they are the spouse that has left. This can be a sensible idea if it helps your husband 'feel' better about the divorce. Legally, it doesn't matter who divorces who, nor does it have any bearing on the financial settlement.

Agree to the 'facts' of your divorce

When you think about divorce, you might think back to the infamous scene when Den left Angie on the Christmas Day episode of Eastenders in 1986. Den, the infamous landlord of the local pub, handed his wife the divorce petition with the immortal words "Happy Christmas Ange!". Now I'm not a soap watcher but I know about this because it's gone down in TV history. Did you know that a record 30.15 million people watched that episode?! In reality, divorce is rarely like that. If you want to save time and money in your divorce, you'd be wise not to issue papers in that way!

If it is possible, agree with your husband that there will be a divorce. Don't spring it upon him unless to do otherwise is unsafe for you. You see, agreeing to divorce and the facts you will rely on will save you time and money. If you wish, you can agree the wording of the divorce petition. Yes, you did read that right: you can sit down and discuss what will appear in the papers. Agreeing in advance who will divorce who and what the papers will say will make it so much easier. Perhaps now you'll see why communication is important during your divorce.

What does divorce actually do?

The only thing that divorce does is end your marriage. That's it. It doesn't resolve anything relating to your finances or arrangements for your children. It's so important that you understand this. In my role as a family mediator, I sometimes work with couples who have long been divorced. Perhaps 20 years or more. They tell me that they decided to divorce, so they sold the house and split the proceeds of sale and their cash in a way that they were content with at the time. They did the divorce themselves and didn't use a lawyer. Sounds good doesn't it? Yes? Well no actually. You see in order for you to be financially free from your obligations, you need a financial remedy order. Now, if you remarry after divorce, you may not make a claim for spousal maintenance, but any claims that were 'live' in the divorce petition can still be made even when you're divorced – the same goes for your former husband. Seek legal advice about this as to how it may impact upon you. But what if your ex-husband doesn't remarry? If he doesn't remarry and you haven't legally resolved your financial obligations, you may be pursued financially in later years for anything that was outlined in the divorce petition.

Get your finances resolved now. Even if you believe that your husband is about to 'strike it rich' which, let's face it, doesn't happen to many, you will also need to have been married for quite a time for you to be entitled to some of that money, so why wait? It could be that in waiting, you also come into money and may have to share it with your ex-husband. Waiting doesn't really achieve anything. If you're unsure about this, for example a substantial inheritance is pending, seek legal advice.

Ladies like you are often nervous of working out their finances because it's daunting at best, and scary at worst, but it doesn't get easier, it just gets later. The sooner you begin to get to grips with your numbers, the sooner you'll begin to deal with the reality of your situation, and the sooner you can start planning your new life with the financial skills you need to move forward as a single woman.

Do I need a lawyer?

Not every lady who gets divorced needs a lawyer. It really depends on your individual circumstances, how well you communicate and how complicated your situation is. However, it's fair to say that most people do benefit from getting legal advice. The type of circumstance which would lend itself to you not needing a lawyer would be that you have been married for a short period of time (five years or less), you do not have significant assets such as property, neither do you have pensions. You don't have children. In this scenario, it's likely that you will keep what you had when you came into the marriage and divide any cash between you. You would still be wise to have a financial consent order drawn up to ensure that no future claims are made against you if you were to come into money in the future. If you have been married for longer than five years, own property, have investments, pensions and debt, or you can't agree how you will manage your children, you will be wise to seek legal advice.

This does not mean that you need to spend a fortune hiring the most expensive lawyer. The most expensive lawyer is not necessarily the best lawyer for you. City centre lawyers charge a lot of money not because they are better necessarily, but because they have greater overheads – remember that you pay for this.

When choosing a lawyer, take your time. Find an expert family lawyer – your friend who is a conveyancing expert or an employment lawyer who is giving you advice for free over a coffee is NOT the right person for you, however nice, friendly and helpful they are. If the person who is giving you advice is not willing to give that advice in writing as your lawyer, they aren't your lawyer!

Your lawyer is going to be a significant part of your divorce process. You need to feel able to trust them and to be able to communicate with them. Do your homework, call a few and talk to them directly. Take advice from people that you know and trust.

Consider using a lawyer who is collaboratively trained or a mediator even if you don't use those processes. Why? Because you'll have a fair idea that these lawyers have a genuine desire to resolve conflicts, saving you time, money and heartache.

I always recommend lawyers who are members of Resolution: www.resolution.org.uk. Resolution lawyers are trained and sign up to its code of conduct to avoid conflict and court proceedings as much as possible. Resolution lawyers believe that, in the vast majority of cases, court proceedings can be avoided. This does not guarantee that your case will not end up in court. It might. Also remember, even if your case is listed for a contested hearing, your lawyers should be negotiating throughout the process meaning that it is unlikely that your case will get to final hearing.

Angela and Katie

Neither Angela nor Katie had instructed lawyers when we began to work together. They found it useful to get clear about their own desires and to understand the divorce process and what was about to happen before they instructed lawyers.

Like most people, both Angela and Katie needed independent legal advice. I explored with Angela and Katie the options available to them and how to find a lawyer who would meet their needs.

Angela and Katie took this information and found lawyers with whom they felt comfortable, and who understood what they wanted in their divorce. Both ladies shared those choices with me and we discussed what it was about their particular lawyers that they liked.

We carried on working together alongside the legal process – that's where divorce coaching works best. Angela and Katie had already covered significant ground both emotionally and practically by the time their lawyers were instructed, allowing them to feel in control and confident.

Applying for divorce

The divorce petition

To apply for a divorce in England and Wales, visit www.gov.uk/divorce. There you'll find all the forms you need, and an up-to-date list of the current costs of each application. I have not included the costs of the application nor the names of the forms here because they change from time to time. Visit www.gov.uk/divorce/overview for links to current paperwork and costs. You can also visit bit.ly/Howtobealadywholeavesbookresources for a list of up-to-date form names and a flow chart to assist you.

If you're the person applying for a divorce, you are the petitioner and you must complete the divorce petition. If you're going to fill in the form for your husband (many of my clients do this), you will be known as the respondent. The petition (along with all other court forms) has an accompanying set of guidance notes to assist you with the completion. You may find it very straightforward, and you can pay for legal help to assist with this if you wish.

In order to apply for your divorce, you will need your original marriage certificate. Start to look for it now if you're not sure where it is. If you cannot find it, you can apply for a copy from the General Register Office http://www.gro.gov.uk/gro/content/certificates. Your application will not be accepted by the court without it. If you got married abroad, you will need a copy of that certificate and a certified copy of its translation. Again, you must have these certificates before you apply for your divorce.

About the petition

The petition will ask you for the details of both you and your husband including an address for service of the petition upon him or you, if you are going to be the respondent. If you do not know where your husband is, you may need to employ a tracing service to help you find him. This is so he can be served with the divorce petition (see **My husband has failed to respond** below). You also need to give the details of all your children even if they are now adults. Remember to tick the boxes to show that you are legally entitled to apply for a divorce in England or Wales (see above in relation to domicile and a habitual residence test). If you are still unsure about this, seek legal advice.

The form will also ask you to state which of the 'five facts' you wish to rely on for your divorce. See above in relation to the five facts. Once you have completed the form, send the original and a copy to the court. Keep a set for yourself. You will also be required to pay the requisite fee at this time. Visit www.gov.uk to find out whether you can claim a fee exemption. If you are not entitled to any fee exemption, the full fee shall be payable by you, the petitioner. In reality, it doesn't matter who pays the fee, so long as it is paid.

Divorce centres

All divorce centres in England and Wales were centralised in December 2015. This may mean that your local county court will no longer accept applications for divorce. Visit www.gov.uk to find out your nearest centre or contact your local county court for guidance.

What happens next?

On receipt of your divorce petition, the court will check and process it and send a copy to your husband at the address you provided. An acknowledgement of service document form and a notice of proceedings will accompany the petition. You will receive a copy of this too. Your husband has eight days to sign and return the form. Remember that if you and your husband have been able to discuss getting divorced, this will not come as a surprise to him and it should mean that he responds immediately. If this has not been possible, and your husband wishes to contest the divorce, he has a further 14 days to file a response (see **My husband has failed to respond** below) if you have not had a response from your husband.

The acknowledgement of service

The acknowledgement of service asks a series of straightforward questions including whether or not your husband agrees to divorce. Your husband should return this form (if you are the respondent you should return the form) stating that he is content to divorce. If your husband intends to defend the divorce he'll state his reasons on this form.

Statement of case

You will need to complete a 'statement of allegations' outlining which of the five facts you wish to rely on. Your husband will see this. Remember that I said it is useful if you and your husband can agree the wording in advance? Well this is why. You do not need to give chapter and verse here; keep it simple, and keep as much emotion out of it as you possibly can. Focus on the facts. If you are relying on the grounds of adultery, keep it brief. Stick to the facts. If you are relying on unreasonable behaviour, use a handful of examples. Your husband does not have to make any admissions; he can merely accept the statement allegations.

The decree nisi

If the court is satisfied that all the correct paperwork has been received from both you and your husband, you may apply for a decree nisi. The decree nisi is a document that basically means that the court does not see any reason why you cannot be divorced. If you both agree to divorce, you will not need to attend a hearing. If your husband disagrees, you will have to go to court and a judge will decide whether to grant you the decree. You will also need to complete the Statement in Support of Divorce (in versions A-E depending on the fact you are relying on), outlining one of the five facts mentioned above. You will have to sign a statement of truth. You will also be required to sign to confirm that the signature on the acknowledgement of service is that of your husband.

Once you have completed the Statement in Support, sign and send it back to the court with the application for the decree nisi. Do not return this form to the court until nine days after your husband has said that he has received the application. You will need to attach the acknowledgement of service showing your husband has received all paperwork and accepts that there should be a divorce.

If the judge is satisfied you can have a divorce the court will send you and your husband a certificate of entitlement to decree nisi. It will tell you the date that the judge will pronounce the decree nisi. You do not need to attend court on that date.

If the judge refuses to grant you the decree nisi, you'll be sent a refusal letter. This letter tells you why the judge has decided that, at the present time, an order can't be granted and what further information is needed. You may also be required to attend a hearing.

What should I do if my husband wishes to defend the divorce?

Your husband will be required, if he wishes to defend the divorce, to file an 'Answer'. There will be a fee for this. He will complete a form and return it to the court. Your husband has 21 days after seven working days of receiving the petition in which to file his answer. This means 28 days from him receiving your petition. You must therefore wait 29 days from the date that your husband says he received the petition before you can apply for the decree nisi. This period may be longer if it falls on a bank holiday. If you do not receive an answer from your husband after this period, you may apply for the decree nisi, asking the court for a 'case management hearing' (there's a fee for this). The judge will decide whether to grant you the decree nisi or not.

My husband has failed to respond – what do I do?

If your husband fails to return the acknowledgement of service eight days after you have sent the petition, you may get two copies from the court of a request for bailiff service. If you can, consider using a process server – they work longer hours than court bailiffs and you are likely to get a faster result. You will need to include a photograph or written description of your husband with a view to service. You may also apply for the court to consider deemed service or to dispense with service if you have done all you can to attempt to locate him. There will be a fee for this.

Costs

On application for divorce you may ask the court to consider awarding costs against your husband if you are the petitioner. This is particularly relevant if you were applying on the facts of adultery, unreasonable behaviour or desertion. However, you can still agree to pay your own costs if you wish, and often this is easier. You do not have to pursue your husband for costs and this is part of the pre-divorce conversation that you can have. If you are divorcing on the grounds of separation it is usual for you to pay your own costs.

Today, it's more and more common for divorcing spouses to combine all costs and split them equally, particularly if you both want the divorce and it's to everyone's benefit.

I now have my decree nisi; am I divorced?

No. The decree nisi is an indication by the courts that legally it sees no reason why you should not be divorced. But at this stage, you are still legally married and are under no obligation to get divorced. You may change your mind at any time prior to the pronouncement of the decree absolute.

The decree absolute

Six weeks and one day after the decree nisi has been pronounced, the petitioner may apply for the decree absolute. The decree absolute is the document which formally ends your marriage. If the petitioner does not apply for the decree absolute the respondent i.e. your husband may apply 12 weeks after the six week and one day period. He would be required to give you notice of his intention to apply. You should apply for your decree absolute within 12 months of the announcement of the decree nisi or you will have to explain the delay to the court.

The period in between the decree nisi and the decree absolute

The minimum period of six weeks and one day between decree nisi and decree absolute usually takes longer. Why? Because after the pronouncement of your decree nisi, the court has the power to begin to consider a financial remedy order. As mentioned above, it is preferable to resolve financial matters whilst you're still married. It is usual then for the decree absolute to be delayed until a financial remedy order has been agreed. This is the reason why you often hear that divorce takes more than a year. It isn't the divorce itself that takes the time; it's the negotiations over the financial remedy order that cause the delay.

Family mediation

I mentioned above that divorce just ends your marriage, and that your financial situation and your children are separate issues. Since 2011, in order to apply to the court for either a financial remedy order or a court order in respect of your children (whether you're married or not), you must meet with a family mediator.

Angela

Angela was keen to use family mediation, and this was supported by her lawyer. Michael chose the mediator and they attended a few sessions. Both Angela and Michael found it challenging but they were able to begin financial discussions. Michael's reticence to divorce, however, thwarted mediation because he began to drift. Michael had not yet instructed a lawyer and Angela felt that Michael was merely paying lip service to the process. She found it very frustrating. After a few sessions of mediation, that Angela felt went nowhere, she issued divorce proceedings.

Angela was disappointed with this as her desire had been to agree financial matters with Michael before proceedings were issued.

Mediation is always a choice and sometimes, no matter how much it makes sense, it doesn't work!

As a family mediator myself, I can say with good authority that it is a good choice for most people, but it's not for everyone. There are limited legal exceptions to the need to meet with a family mediator, the main one being domestic abuse situations. There may be some of you who have experienced domestic abuse that may feel able to use family mediation. You can talk with a mediator about this.

The fact that you don't want to mediate doesn't preclude you from having to go to see a mediator. Equally, family mediation isn't suitable for many complex financial cases but you'll still need to visit a mediator to have your mediation information and assessment meeting (MIAM). A MIAM is a meeting between you and a mediator to discuss how mediation may help you. You may decide mediation isn't for you and/or the mediator may decide that mediation isn't suitable for you, even if you want to use it.

Rachel and Bob

It's important that I share the story of Rachel and Bob with you so that you understand the power of a family mediation. I worked with Rachel and Bob in my capacity as a family mediator, not as a divorce coach. My colleague Chris and I met Rachel and Bob some two years after their initial separation and 12 months into their divorce.

Rachel and Bob had been trying to negotiate a financial settlement through their lawyers and could not reach agreement. Rachel was angry and hurt by Bob's infidelity. Rachel only became aware of Bob's new relationship when he moved out of the family home that he shared with Rachel and their two children. Rachel was also worried about having financial security.

Since their separation, Rachel and Bob had barely spoken. Their joint legal fees totalled £24,000 and they'd got nowhere. Mediation allowed them to come together. It was painful and challenging at times. Anger, tears, regrets and apologies flowed. Mediation allowed them to focus on their children's needs and their own futures rather than looking at the past. Rachel and Bob came to five mediation sessions over a period of just under six months. Proposals were agreed that they could both accept. Financially and emotionally they were both able to move forward to ask the court for consent order. **The joint cost of mediation was less than £4,000.**

As a mediator, I'm in favour of separating couples bringing their unresolved issues to mediation. Mediation gives you the freedom to say what you want in a way the court process does not. The fact that you don't want to mediate doesn't prevent you from having to go to see a mediator.

Mediation helps you and your husband to communicate and make decisions about money and/or your children. You decide what you want to talk about, not a mediator. Your mediator will give you legal information but not legal advice. Legal information includes outlining the law, what it says and how it works. Legal advice is a stage further. For example, saying "and so Mrs Smith, my advice is that you should seek a settlement of £X" would be giving you legal advice. Mediators (even if they are lawyers), are not allowed to give you legal advice. You can, of course, use a lawyer to support the mediation process, by discussing the proposals you make in mediation with them and to decide whether those proposals should form the basis of a consent order.

Mediation is the place to test options and possibilities. Mediation is confidential and is not legally binding. Only if you reach an agreement that you both want to be legally binding will you then ask a lawyer to draft the consent order. The consent order is legally binding. So you see, you have plenty of time to explore options, get legal advice and future pace (see **Divorce coaching** in Section 6). The benefits are that you use your lawyers less because there are less letters, phone calls and emails sent between you and your husband's lawyer so it saves you money and time. It is also beneficial because you are supported to communicate with your husband which is particularly important if you have children together because as much as you may not want to admit it, you will have to have a co-parenting relationship once your divorce is finalised.

What happens at the end of mediation?

If you and your husband reach agreement in the mediation process, the mediator will draw up a document called a Memorandum of Understanding or MOU. The MOU is a document which outlines the principles by which you have mediated, for example to be fair to each other and put your children first, and the decisions you have made in relation to your assets and liabilities on that basis. You may take this document to your lawyer to get legal advice. This document is not legally binding and may be changed. It will be drafted in such a way that it will be straightforward for a lawyer to draft a consent order based on its contents.

Who are mediators?

Mediators may be lawyers or non-lawyers. Whether you choose a lawyer mediator or a non-lawyer mediator is entirely a matter for you. Non-lawyer mediators tend to be relationship counsellors, family therapists, social workers, family consultants, psychotherapists or people with a general interest in social relationships. Ensure that you find an accredited mediator. Then you can be sure that they have proper training, accreditation and insurance. There are many good non-lawyer mediators, however I would recommend that if you have financial matters to discuss, you will benefit from using a lawyer mediator who will have experience of negotiating such matters to trial. Whilst they will not be able to give you legal advice, they will be able to give you more detailed information about your situation and how it is likely to be dealt with by a court. They will also be more alive to the complexities of your case and be able to further guide you as to other professionals you need to speak to.

You may wish to choose a mediator with experience of working with children if you have complex child-related issues to resolve.

The costs of mediation

The costs of family mediation vary across the country. Some central London mediators charge the same for their mediation services as they do for their legal advice. Other mediation services including lawyer mediators charge substantially less. You really do get what you pay for! On average, however, the costs of family mediation are significantly less than using lawyers exclusively. The costs will be determined by the number of sessions that you need. Each case is of course individual. However, an average of three to five sessions is standard. Much will depend on how far into the financial process you are at the start of the mediation, how detailed and complex your financial circumstances, and how easy the two of you find discussing your issues.

Many not-for-profit organisations exist which charge substantially less than lawyer mediators for their services. You will find these locally. Some organisations offer mediation on a fixed fee basis, while others charge by the hour or by the session.

Public funding

Public funding or legal aid is available for mediation. It is only available for divorce proceedings in a very limited number of circumstances. This is why mediation is a good option if you are on a low income, because you will currently get some support with the process either at a reduced rate or, if you qualify for public funding, free.

Even if you own property, you may be entitled to public funding. It depends upon your disposable income. If you qualify for certain means tested benefits, you may automatically be 'passported' for public funding save for any capital assets which you have. Capital assets include savings, cash in your current account, paintings, vintage cars and jewellery by way of example. If you have (currently) over £8,000 of savings (even if that's the proceeds of the sale of your house) you will not be entitled to public funding even if you are on benefits. If you are earning, if you exceed the current gross monthly income figure you will not be entitled to public funding either. As these figures are subject to change please visit https://www.gov.uk/check-legal-aid to see whether you qualify for public funding. If you qualify for public funding your husband will also receive a free MIAM and the first session of mediation free. Contact a local mediation provider for further information.

Divorce process options

One of the things that many of my clients are not aware of is the availability of different methods of approaching their divorce.

The traditional court process

The traditional court process is the one you'll be most familiar with. You go and find a lawyer, and your husband finds a lawyer. You seek advice from your lawyer and your husband gets advice from his lawyer. Your lawyers (acting on your instructions) begin the negotiating process for you. One of them may file the divorce petition or you may do this yourself. Your lawyers may deal with issuing a response and beginning financial negotiations. This might be because you don't want to do it yourself, or because it's not safe for you to do so. In the traditional court process if you do not wish to speak to your husband you do not have to – your lawyers will do it all for you. You may think that sounds perfect, but the thing is it's expensive. The average cost of the family lawyer is approximately £200 per hour. They bill in six minute units for every piece of work, phone calls, emails, or letters sent by you, or received on your behalf by your lawyer from your husband or his lawyer. You are charged for everything. When you're feeling emotional it's not always easy to remember that, and the cost of your divorce can quickly spiral without any real progress being made.

Your lawyer may work by offering you a fixed fee package. Fixed fee packages aren't suitable for everyone. There are advantages and disadvantages of using them. Fixed fee packages tell you upfront what you'll get by way of service for the fee you pay. If you are interested in this, ensure that you are clear about exactly what is included and what is excluded. You pay extra for those things that are outside the fixed fee agreement.

As *The Family Court Statistics Quarterly for England & Wales*, published on 31st March 2016, shows, there were 9,062 applications for financial remedy between October and December 2016. Of these 65% were uncontested (agreed). Of these 26% were initially contested but resolved, and 9% were contested throughout. Just because a case starts off contested does not mean there won't be opportunities for negotiation and settlement throughout. So using the traditional court process does not mean that you will end up in court.

Costs

The costs of your divorce will vary according to the complexity of your circumstances, the ability of each of you to manage the process and the hourly rate of your lawyer. If you prepare well, understand the process, understand what's possible for you and have a good handle on your emotions, divorce could cost you around £1,500 each (this includes court fees, MIAM, consent order drawing up and a session of mediation). Many financial remedy applications start contested but settle.

If you end up in a contested situation, an average cost may be £8–£10,000 each. If you live in a big city it's likely to be higher. Often, it is significantly more – £20–£30,000 is not unreasonable if you have substantial assets and you are unable to compromise.

Sadly, not all lawyers want to save you money. Creating conflict and encouraging you to pursue matters you're not interested in are the ways they make their fees. This is why finding the right lawyer for you is important. Not all lawyers encourage conflict, however!

Collaborative law

Have you heard of collaborative law? Possibly not. Collaborative law is very similar to the mediation process except the main difference is that your lawyer is with you. Collaborative lawyers are specially trained to avoid conflict and to help you reach a compromised agreement. If you decide to use the collaborative process each of you will find a collaboratively trained lawyer. Initially you will have a meeting on your own with your lawyer. You will then have round table meetings – you and your lawyer with your husband and his lawyer. These meetings are known as 'four-way meetings'.

At the first meeting with your lawyer, you will discuss what you would like to achieve from the collaborative process. Your lawyer and your husband's lawyer will then plan your four-way meeting. You will draw up a document called a participation agreement. Your participation agreement is unique to you and outlines the principles by which you wish to negotiate such as being open minded and fair – it's your commitment to the process. You will also draw up a document known as an anchor statement. This is a statement of what the two of you hope to achieve through the collaborative process and it keeps you focused on the 'real' issues that you have to discuss. You will be reminded of these principles throughout the collaborative process if you and your husband begin to struggle.

This first session will also outline the background to your relationship and your family situation. At your second session, it is likely that you will begin to look at your financial situation, your income and expenses, housing needs, assets and liabilities. Once each of you is clear about this a further session will look at how to deal with all of these in line with the principles set out in your participation agreement. A final meeting may be needed to clarify the agreement that you wish to make. Depending on the complexity of your case, you may need more than four sessions, but you may also need less.

Other professionals such as family consultants, pensions advisors or accountants may also be invited to the sessions in order to help with the negotiations for a financial settlement and arrangements for your children. By using the collaborative process, each of you must agree that you will not issue proceedings.

If you and your husband do not reach agreement under the collaborative process, you will have to find new lawyers as the lawyers who have supported you through the collaborative process are not allowed to represent you in a contested hearing.

Costs

The cost of the collaborative process will depend on how many sessions you and your husband have. However, when the collaborative process works well it saves you both time and money because you're able to resolve matters more quickly. Not only does the collaborative process save you money but it also helps you to move through the communication difficulties that you may be experiencing with your husband.

The collaborative process is not the cheapest process but it can achieve quick results. If being actively involved in negotiations rather than being a spectator appeals to you, the collaborative process is worth considering.

Arbitration

Family arbitration is a relatively new dispute resolution tool in England and Wales. It is different from both the mediation and collaborative process. An arbitrator is trained to make final decisions for you about the property or finances when you cannot make them yourself. The decision of an arbitrator is binding. You may use an arbitrator if you find yourself in a situation where the majority of your finances have been agreed but there is one outstanding matter that needs resolution, or you may use an arbitrator to help you resolve all of your property and finance issues. Using arbitration is often much quicker and less formal than going to court. In this way, it can save you money.

Although you hand over the decision-making to an arbitrator, you do retain control in a number of respects. You get to choose your arbitrator. You can find out more about how to choose an arbitrator at http://www.ifla.org.uk. This means that you can choose an arbitrator with specialist skills in an area that you need. You get to decide how financial disclosure is dealt with (see Section 4 **Financial disclosure** below). Using the court process, you will complete the Form E. In arbitration, you can use this form if you wish, but if you decide to use your own spreadsheet or an A4 piece of paper, so long as the two of you agree, you may do this. Arbitration is therefore more flexible than the court process.

Arbitration may not be suitable in cases where you need a judge to make orders that an arbitrator cannot. For example, an arbitrator cannot make an order freezing assets, nor can they make an order for the return of property. However, should you need to ask a court for orders such as these in the arbitration process, you can do so and then return to arbitration. If you feel that your husband is hiding assets, arbitration is unlikely to be suitable for you.

Once you have chosen an arbitrator, and you have agreed to be bound by the process, you cannot back out of it unless both of you agree. Together you will decide what you want the arbitrator to rule on. The arbitrator will use the law of England and Wales upon which to base their decision, having heard representations from each of you. These may be written, done over the telephone or via face-to-face meetings; you get to choose. Once the arbitrator has made a decision they will notify you in writing giving their reasons. Their decision is legally binding and can only be challenged if it is wrong in law. Once you have their decision, you ask the court to ratify it in a court order.

You may still use your lawyers to guide you through the arbitration process as you might in mediation.

Costs

The cost of family arbitration varies across the country. You will agree the fees of the arbitrator usually on an hourly basis though fixed fees may be available. Whilst it is true that you do not pay a judge to make an order on your divorce, savings can be made by using an arbitrator because although you need to pay for it, the only limitation on time is that of yourselves, the arbitrator and your legal advisers.

On reaching agreement – the consent order

The consent order is the legally binding document which outlines the decisions you have made in respect of your finances. For example, what happens to the family home, cash pensions and other assets you may have. We will look in more detail at these issues in the finances section.

A consent order is legally binding and can rarely be changed.

What if we don't reach agreement?

If you don't reach agreement, your case will proceed towards a court hearing. Remember, although the court hearings follow a schedule, you and your husband may reach agreement and settle at any time – most cases do. Visit bit.ly/ Howtobealadywholeavesbookresources to access the most up-to-date worksheets on financial remedy hearings.

Section 4

Finances

Introduction

Now that you have turned the page and you've seen that this section is about your finances, you may have a very heavy heart? Alternatively, you might be one of those ladies who has a really good grasp of their financial situation. It doesn't necessarily follow, however, that you feel confident about dealing with finances on divorce.

You've probably heard lots of horror stories about how much divorce costs, about how ladies end up with nothing, or with everything. Both positions are often exaggerated either by the media or the storyteller themselves. It's important to remember that the divorce rate in England and Wales in 2014 was just less than 113,000. That's a lot of divorces. We don't know how each of those matters proceeded. Remember that the press enjoys the drama of the headline cases. Are you a headline case? Well it's not for me to say, but it's unlikely.

You will recall that I said it's not the divorce process itself that takes time; it's usually the financial matters that delay divorce. In this section, we'll be looking at the elements of a financial remedy order. Remember that the financial remedy order is separate to divorce. However, the proceedings will most likely run alongside. This protects your position and saves you time. We'll be looking at how to prepare for financial disclosure, why it's important to understand your own financial position, why it is important to understand what you need, and the steps that you can take to avoid lengthy disagreements with your husband over money. Can I guarantee that you won't end up in court? No! Not even your lawyer can guarantee that. There are however many things that you can do to lessen the likelihood of that happening. Of course, you're not in control of your husband, or the legal advice that he receives.

Remember that money is a very emotive issue. It may seem at this stage that you and your husband are getting along quite amicably, even though you are separating. You may be less inclined on that basis to do anything about your finances. This can be a very naive attitude. You have no control over who your husband talks to and what barrack-room legal advice he's getting down the pub. Equally, it could only take one disagreement between you (that may have nothing to do with money), for you to find the current account is empty and all the credit cards maxed out. Now I'm not saying that this is going to happen, but you would be foolish not to consider it. Money can make even the most rational of people crazy. Money makes people fearful and behave out of character. For this reason, I often recommend to my clients that even if they haven't decided to divorce yet, they begin to start gathering the information that they will need for financial disclosure before telling their husband. This may feel underhand. Let me make it clear, I'm not suggesting that you go and snoop into accounts which you do not legally have access to; don't do this. I'm talking about the accounts to which you do have access, which will include your own accounts and joint accounts. Gathering this information will support you to be clear about what you have.

If you feel that your husband is likely to start hiding money or move it into a foreign jurisdiction, you may need to seek legal advice about getting a court order to freeze your assets. There is no point in you taking copies of documents which are not in your joint names to a lawyer as they can do nothing with them. If you find accounts you knew nothing of, simply make a note of the account numbers and seek legal advice.

Financial disclosure

Before reaching a financial settlement upon divorce, you and your husband will be encouraged to undertake full and frank financial disclosure of all your assets (including pensions), liabilities (debts) and income. Even if you and your husband reach agreement between you, without ever using the services of a lawyer, only the court can make your agreement legally binding. The court will not make a financial remedy order upon divorce, unless disclosure has taken place. So, what financial information is required? Ultimately, the level to which you wish to disclose your financial circumstances is a matter for you and your husband. At the very least, the court requires a statement of information from each of you outlining your financial position. Further, you can agree to limit the detail that each of you discloses. For most people, however, full disclosure is necessary and desirable.

Full disclosure allows each of you to see the assets and the liabilities that each of you have and also the assets and liabilities of the marriage. This is done on the form known as the Form E. The Form E requires detailed information and supporting evidence of your assets, liabilities and income. You will be sharing 12 months' worth of all bank accounts (current and savings), investments, shares, trust funds, pensions, property values and the like. You will also share details of outstanding credit card debts, loans, mortgages etc. Whether you choose to do a statement of information or the full Form E, you will be required to sign a statement of truth, declaring that the document is accurate. Should you or your husband be found to have provided inaccurate information, you may find yourself being charged with contempt of court. This is punishable by a fine or imprisonment.

Whether you need legal advice to assist you with disclosure will depend on several factors. Firstly, how confident and financially astute you are in respect of the family finances. If it was you who dealt with all the finances, you may feel comfortable and well equipped to deal with financial disclosure. If, on the other hand, your husband was the one who managed all your money, you may feel overwhelmed and out of your depth. It will also depend upon how complex your financial arrangements are.

Even when you feel capable, it is often advisable to seek legal advice to support you around disclosure. Experienced lawyers are used to working through the Form E and uncovering genuine oversights by one spouse or attempts to conceal financial information. It is also useful to use a lawyer to give you advice about the extent to which you challenge the financial information provided by your husband. Particularly when you may be feeling emotional, an independent viewpoint can save you a significant amount of time and money. Remember that in challenging your husband's financial disclosure, you will be causing delay and increasing cost. There may be a very good reason for doing this, but sometimes the difference that it makes does not outweigh the cost of doing it. Sometimes it's just better to let things go. Remember also the emotional cost of withholding financial information. Such behaviour causes resentment, suspicion and anxiety, and it does little to ingratiate yourself with your husband. If you have children, remember that their needs must be taken account of, both emotionally and financially. If you have children, you and your husband are going to have to have a continuing relationship of some kind.

So what happens if an order is made and it transpires that one party lied about their assets? The making of a court order does not end a court's power over a marriage. Generally speaking, once an order is made, it is made and it's difficult to ask the courts to revisit it. However, in the case of fraud, it is possible for the court to reopen an order if there has been material non-disclosure, such that no reasonable person, on the facts, would have consented to an order in those terms being made, or that the court would not have made an order in those terms if the truth had been before it. This means that if you deceive the court in such a way that they may have made a different order, the order might be reopened. This will be expensive.

Financial disclosure is the basis of your financial negotiations. You should never negotiate a settlement without having exchanged disclosure. Financial disclosure allows you to know your numbers. You will understand your numbers, his numbers and the numbers in the marriage. Many ladies I work with, either as a divorce coach or a family mediator, come to the negotiating table without having a clear idea of what these numbers are. It's one of the biggest mistakes that you can make on divorce. Know your numbers before you negotiate!

Getting organised

When I work with clients around their financial situation, one of the first things that I encourage them to do is get organised. Why? Well really it's quite simple. You see, even if the divorce is your idea, even if you're absolutely certain that you want to leave, there will be times when you will not feel great, when your brain will be fried, when you haven't a clue what you're doing and you couldn't make a rational decision if your life depended on it. Is that because you're weak and incapable? No, it's because you're a human being. Even if it feels highly unlikely now, trust me when I say this and follow the process of getting organised. You really will thank me; my clients always do!

So what does getting organised look like? The truth is, applying for a financial remedy order is a lot of paperwork. At times, you'll question it and feel like you're drowning. Being organised is the antidote to that feeling of overwhelm and panic. When you decide to get organised ahead of time, you can do it at your pace. Some of this paperwork may take several weeks to come through.

The more relaxed you are when you begin to get organised, the easier it will be. You will feel more in control, you'll be more open to possibilities and you will likely be more proactive.

Angela

Angela and Katie both understood their net worth, which made understanding the financial aspects of the divorce process easy for them in some respects. It was still scary for them, but in different ways.

Angela was the main breadwinner, earned a good salary and had built a large pension prior to meeting her husband. Angela was concerned that she remain in the family home so that her daughter would have stability. She was also concerned that her husband should be able to afford to buy a property nearby so that he could continue to be actively involved in their daughter's life. Ensuring that this could happen was of great concern to Angela. She found gathering the financial documents straightforward. This made it easier to look at all the possibilities. Angela also began to look for an even better paid job with longer hours to ensure that both she and her husband would be able to maintain a similar standard of living on divorce.

Getting organised allowed Angela to feel confident that she could make plans and manage her financial situation as best she could. We chatted around various options available to her and Michael. This allowed Angela to put proposals to Michael so he could feel part of the decision-making process.

Katie

Katie's situation was slightly different. Like Angela, Katie understood her numbers very well. Unlike Angela, however, Katie was not 'earning' any money. Although Katie wasn't working, she'd grown a successful property portfolio using redundancy money from her banking career as well as her husband's earnings.

This made Katie feel insecure, however, because Will repeatedly told her that she didn't work or earn any money. Katie was terrified that Will would cut her off financially at any time. It was incredibly stressful for Katie.

Even though Katie and Will had separated, Will continued to rely on Katie to manage his financial affairs. This stood Katie in good stead because in completing financial disclosure, she knew more about her husband's finances than he did!

Whilst Katie was stressed and incredibly concerned, we worked together to look at the reality of the situation. Managing her husband's threats and controlling behaviour was balanced against the reality of her legal position – that she understood her husband's finances and that the **s25 MCA 1973** factors (mentioned in Section 3) would support her.

Katie was concerned that Will was focused on splitting the capital assets without focusing on the income generating nature of these assets, which Katie had been reliant upon. Will wasn't focusing on the Capital Gains Tax that would be payable either now or at some point in the future and that Katie wouldn't be in a position to apply for her own mortgage as she wasn't earning. Will also failed to take account of his huge salary, the fact that Katie did a greater share of the childcare, and he accused her of being greedy.

Katie spent hours prior to the issuing of the divorce petition working on options for settlement that she and Will could discuss. His continual threats meant that in the end Katie issued proceedings, but she continued to work towards a negotiated settlement with Will.

The Form E

Getting organised will mean that filling in the Form E will be easier. It's important to know what your capital and income needs are. Capital needs are those such as the ability to buy a new home or another car, for example. Your income needs are those which will support you day to day and also provide you with an income to invest so that you can support yourself in the future. Remember that you will need to consider the impact of inflation and taxation because these will influence your numbers.

Remember that your husband will also be required to prepare the Form E. You and your lawyer will consider this form, and you will be able (just as he will with you) to ask questions about what he has put on the form.

Financial statements

A word about financial statements. If you use mediation early on in your divorce, you may complete financial statements rather than Form E. Don't worry about this. Often financial statements are easier to complete. If you have already completed Form E, you can take that to mediation.

Getting to know your numbers

The process of getting to know your numbers doesn't need to be scary. And being organised will make it so much easier. Visit bit. ly/Howtobealadywholeavesbookresources for the Figuring out your Divorce Finances financial challenge to help you begin this process – there you'll find workbooks and audios to accompany you in your journey.

I recommend that you start with the assets. Starting with your assets allows you to gain some confidence in this process before you begin to tackle the more complex aspects of financial disclosure.

Remember that your assets include investments you and your husband may have. There may be some very complicated asset arrangements. It's important that you understand what they are and that you get advice about them. You need to be clear about how risky they are and the tax implications. You need to understand how these may provide you with financial security in the future.

Action Point

Let's consider Yvonne's story.

Yvonne

Angela and Katie are ladies who knew their numbers! Both of them understood the value of all the assets and liabilities.

But what if you don't?

Yvonne is married to Ted. Ted is an accountant. Yvonne doesn't do money because that's Ted's job. Yvonne came to me because she knew that she needed to get a handle on the family's financial situation so that she could better understand what a financial settlement might look like for her. She was terrified. Not because she worried that there wouldn't be enough money; Yvonne knew that there would be enough money for both her and her husband because they each have a property. Yvonne was terrified because she knew that her husband would not accept the idea of divorce for financial reasons.

Ted knew that Yvonne didn't really know the numbers, and whilst he doesn't hide them from her, he doesn't seek to educate her about them either. Ted was fearful that Yvonne would leave and therefore didn't want to share this information with her – it was Ted's way of feeling in control, but it pushed Yvonne further away. Yvonne and I spent a day together formulating a plan based on the numbers that she did have available. She was shocked to discover that their children's school fees were costing more per month than the monthly cash income. It's not that the school fees were unaffordable; in Ted's financial plan, they were affordable.

Ted had a complex financial plan which Yvonne didn't truly understand, but she knew enough to know that Ted's plan was not sustainable on divorce.

Looking at what Yvonne wanted most of all, she discovered that what she really wanted was to get out of the marriage. Although Yvonne did not want to leave the family home, she knew that Ted wouldn't leave and therefore if she wanted her freedom, she would need to leave. We looked at what her income needs would be based on rental valuations and the cost of living, allowing the children to spend time both with her and their father.

Yvonne left the session understanding that there was enough money coming in each month to allow this to happen. Within a month, Yvonne had found a house to rent and she moved out of the family home. The separation allowed Yvonne to understand more about the family's financial situation, and to also take control of her own financial life.

Action Point

From reading Yvonne's story, notice how we worked together to understand her numbers and help her gain the confidence to leave. How does Yvonne's experience resonate with you and what can you do to gain the same clarity?

Assets and liabilities

Assets

So, what are assets? Your assets are the things that you have. Your biggest asset if you own one is (usually) your family home. If you and your husband do not own any property you can skip this section. If your husband owns property that you live in, but do not own, you should keep reading.

I'm not going to go into details of the legal aspects of home ownership but suffice to say that if you and your husband own property together, you will own it either as joint tenants or tenants-in-common. Joint tenancy is the most common way of property owning between husband and wife. You both own the property equally. If one of you were to die, the dead spouse's interest in the property would automatically be passed to the surviving one. You may, however, own property as tenants-in-common. Tenants-in-common own specific shares of the property even if that is 50–50. This means that on the death of a spouse, their half of the property doesn't automatically pass to the other one, and they are free to make what other arrangements they choose for that property. You need to know what your interest in the property is. If you're joint tenants, then you automatically have a 50% share in the property. If you're tenants-in-common one of you may own more of the property than the other, but equally, you may own it in 50–50 shares.

If you live in a house that is owned by your husband but not you, it is important that you ensure that you register an interest in the property at the Land Registry. Registering an interest in the property does not mean that you own it, but it will prevent your husband from selling it from under you. A lawyer can help you with this if you need it.

Property

Have you had the matrimonial home valued recently? When I say recently, I mean within the last three months? If you haven't, one of the first things that you need to do is to get the family home valued by a local estate agent. Ideally, you and your husband will instruct three local estate agents to value the property. You and your husband will probably have some idea of what you think the property is worth. Take those valuations and decide between you, if possible, what you think the property might sell for if you were going to put it on the market for sale. I'm not suggesting at this stage that you will put the property on the market; you may not have enough information yet (although you might). But you do need to know what the property is worth. Once you understand what the property is worth, you need to take off any encumbrances. Encumbrances are any first or second mortgages or any charges on the property that will impact upon the equity left if the property were to be sold. For example, if the house is worth £250,000 and you have a mortgage of £100,000 and there's a charge on the property of £20,000 then the equity in property will be £130,000. You'll need to do this for all the properties that you own, remembering that you may also need to consider that Capital Gains Tax may be payable on the sale of property which may affect the equity available to you, if the property is sold. You will also need to take legal costs and estate agents' fees off this figure. These will vary depending upon whereabouts in the country you live.

For example, using the figure of £250,000 above and taking off 2% for estate agents and legal costs, the equity available is reduced to £125,000. Remember that the estate agents' fees come off the selling price, not the equity you receive. So this would be:

$$2\% \times £250{,}000 = £5{,}000$$

$$£250{,}000 - £100{,}000 - £20{,}000 - £5{,}000$$

$$= £125{,}000$$

Cash

Cash includes money in current accounts, savings accounts, ISAs, bonds, stocks and shares, cash stashed in the house, and investment plans. It may take a bit of time to get all this information together.

 *Action Point*

Start to gather information about your assets. Take as much time as you need and break it down into manageable chunks if you need to. Make a list of all the accounts that you have. Once you've listed all accounts, make a note of all the account numbers. Then either go online (if you use online banking) and download your statements, or apply for 12 months of statements for each of the accounts that you have (some banks now charge for this). Also, make enquiries as to what your stocks and shares are worth and all other investments and write this down. If you wish you can download worksheets from my website, bit.ly/ Howtobealadywholeavesbookresources

It could take you anything from a couple of hours to a couple of days to figure out exactly how much cash you have. It may surprise you just how much there is. This is why this is such an important exercise, and why I recommend that ladies who want to leave do this exercise sooner rather than later because in getting organised they're beginning to understand exactly what money they have, so they can feel more confident in the decisions they're going to make. Not only is this exercise necessary for the divorce process, but it is also often the first step to becoming financially savvy, a skill that will support the lady who leaves going forward.

Art, antiques and collectibles

It may surprise you, or even horrify you, that you will be invited to list any art, antiques, collectibles and jewellery that you have that are worth over £500. But before you panic, remember that you and your husband will get to choose what goes into the marital pot. This is initially just an exercise in collating your wealth. You may choose to find it quite useful because often we forget just what we have and how much it's worth. It also may remind you that you need to update your insurance!

Action Point

List everything that you have and its estimated value. Make a note of what is yours, that which you brought to the relationship, what you were given as a gift, what is his or was given to him as a gift, and what you jointly own either by way of gift or because you purchased it together. For some people, this is a necessary exercise because it is a source of capital that needs to be liquidated in order to provide one party with funds. You may be in the fortunate position not to need to worry about this too much. You may not have any particular emotional attachments to any of these items or your husband might be happy for you to keep them. That will be the subject of negotiations further down the line.

Liabilities

Liabilities are the things that you owe. In relation to divorce we often exclude the mortgage at this point because we have looked at it in relation to the equity available in your property. Your liabilities include loans, credit cards, your mobile phone agreement and other credit agreements such as furniture, kitchens and car payments.

Your debts

You are legally responsible for any debts that are purely in your name, irrespective of how the debt accrued. Clear your debt prior to starting your divorce if you can – I know it's not always possible. It may be that as part of your divorce settlement, your husband agrees to give you a lump sum to clear the debt, but technically it is yours to pay. It is common for each of you to agree to pay your own personal debt after the divorce. If you will struggle with this, you may need to take further advice which is detailed below.

Now I have a question for you! Hold on, you might not like it: Does your husband know about all your debts? I mean credit cards, store cards and catalogues? Are they in your name only or joint names? Getting a copy of your credit file will help you get clear about what debt you have.

Joint debts

Joint debts are those which you and your husband have taken out together (whether or not you knew about them). You are 'jointly and severally liable' for these debts. You need to be clear with yourself about which debts are yours and which are joint. In respect of this, which debts are yours and which debts are joint is a matter of fact rather than morality. By this I mean whose name is on the credit agreement. Any credit agreements in a sole name (either yours or his) are the responsibility of the person whose name is on the agreement, irrespective of the purpose of the loan. For example, if a loan was taken out in your name to buy a motorbike for your husband that you have never ridden, the debt is yours. If you both signed the credit agreement, the debt is joint.

Looking at your liabilities can be scary, particularly when you know that you are living beyond your means. The first thing to do is to remind yourself that this exercise is about moving forward. It isn't about blame and guilt. You may find doing this very emotional and that's okay. Be kind and gentle with yourself and remind yourself this is a positive step forward. You will learn so much about yourself, your behaviours and your real needs by doing this. This exercise will help you make smarter decisions; it will help you ask for what you need and also plan for the future.

The thought of doing this may be overwhelming, I understand. If you feel like this, take it step by step. It might be that you take the list of all your liabilities and tackle one at a time. For example, today you might decide to look at all your credit cards and store cards and nothing else. This is fine. If this helps you to stay calm and prevents you from feeling overwhelmed, do it.

 Action Point

» The first thing that you need to do is gather together all the relevant paperwork. This might take a while. Do you have paper statements, or do you need to order or download them? Ensure that you get current redemption figures for your outstanding loans. You will need 12 months' worth of credit card and store card statements if you have them.

» Grab your notebook and pen and find somewhere where you can see all your financial documents. You can use the financial workbooks on my website bit.ly/ Howtobealadywholeavesbookresources to help you. You only need to include the latest figures in the financial statements or the Form E, but it may help you to look through your last 12 months of credit card statements.

» What did you spend your money on? Was it on luxuries or necessities for you and the family? Having this knowledge is crucial. Depending on your lifestyle and the overall asset base, you may be able to continue spending on luxuries if you use your credit card as a means of payment which is cleared at the end of every month. If however you are living off your credit cards because there isn't enough cash to survive on, the picture may be very different and you may be looking at a very different lifestyle. This can be emotionally very hard and this exercise is not designed to upset you, but the sooner that you can come face to face with the reality of the situation, the sooner that you will be able to begin to come to terms with it and make sensible decisions.

Continue this exercise until you have completed the liability section of your statement. At the bottom, you'll be able to work out exactly what you owe. Some of this liability may be yours alone. Without agreement to the contrary, you will be expected to pay this. As mentioned before, any joint debt i.e. debt that is both in yours and your husband's name is owned equally by both of you. You will need to ensure that this is paid before you are divorced. Either one of you may be pursued by the loan company if it is not paid.

Your net worth

Now that you are aware just how much you owe, you will be able to take this figure and minus it from your asset figure. This will give you your net worth.

Assets - Liabilities = Net Worth

Trust me when I say that calculating net worth is one of the most important things that you can do in your financial life irrespective of whether you are getting divorced or not, but on divorce, it's crucial. Your net worth tells you exactly where you are financially.

During the financial disclosure process, you will discover your own net worth, the net worth of your husband and that of your marriage.

When your net worth is not going to be enough

Calculating your net worth can be a pleasant surprise for many people because they forget just how many assets they have. However, sometimes calculating your net worth can be devastating. This can be for a number of reasons. It could be that you have known for some time that as a family you are overspending due to underemployment, unemployment, the failure of financial investments, unexpected expenses on property, vet bills or sickness, for example. For others, devastation occurs because one or both parties is totally unaware of the realities of their financial situation. I have worked with women who were unaware that their husbands were taking financial risks without their knowledge. Men who obtained credit in their wives' names without their knowledge. Men who are in charge of the family finances and regularly overspend without their wives being aware. Coming face to face with this reality can be devastating.

So what do you do, when it becomes obvious that there will not be enough money for each of you to start again?

If this is you, don't panic. There is plenty of support to help you. Your local Citizens Advice Bureau is a good place to start. The Money Advice Service may be helpful too. You may find this challenging if you've never had to reach out like this before. Remember that these organisations are there to help you, and not to judge you. Chances are, they have seen and heard it all before and most probably worse.

Action Point

Start by notifying all the relevant providers of your debt of the situation. Discuss putting a hold on all of your accounts so neither of you can run up further debt. Doing so behind your husband's back can be a declaration of war and make things worse, but if it's necessary, do it! Remember that joint and several liability means that each of you can be chased for the whole of the amount outstanding. For example, you and your husband take out a loan for £1,000. You pay back £500 but your husband refuses to pay 'his' share. The loan company are legally entitled to pursue you for the remaining £500 even though you have paid 'your' share.

If you have a credit card account where your husband is a named cardholder only, you are responsible for all the debt even though he has spent the money, so cancel his card immediately.

Remember that the Citizens Advice Bureau and the Money Advice Service can support you with debt counselling. It is outside the scope of this book to go into detail about debt management, but suffice to say that debt counsellors will help you understand the difference between priority and non-priority debts. They will help you approach all your creditors to explain your situation, and to negotiate lower rates of repayment.

Notice of disassociation

Once your marriage has ended, it is important that you formally sever all financial ties between the two of you when you can. It might be that for financial reasons, you will need to continue to be linked to one another, but if you have managed to obtain a clean break, you should cut all financial ties. Obtain a copy of your credit file. This is a sensible way to look at all the links that you and your former husband have. Ensure that the credit file is updated and lodge a notice of disassociation to ensure that current or future lenders do not link your credit file to that of your former husband. You will not be able to do this if financial ties have not been severed completely.

IVA

If your situation is chronic, it may be suggested to you that you enter into an IVA or individual voluntary arrangement. An IVA is managed by an insolvency practitioner. They will support you by negotiating with your creditors regarding how much of the debt you have to pay over a limited period of time, usually five years. At the end of that period, the rest of the debt will be written off. IVAs are expensive, however, and it's not possible to include joint debts because the other person will still be liable for the remainder of the debt at the end of the IVA period.

You will need to consider the effect of an IVA on your credit rating, your home and possessions such as a car. Your credit rating is likely to reduce significantly meaning that getting credit in the future is difficult – the IVA will remain on your credit file for six years from the beginning of the IVA. You may have to remortgage your home at the end of the period and, if you cannot remortgage, may have to sell. Any large possessions such as cars may have to be sold as part of the IVA. In order to apply for an IVA, debts must usually be at least £10,000.

Bankruptcy

What is bankruptcy? Bankruptcy is a legal status which usually lasts for a year but the consequences can be far reaching. Bankruptcy really is a last resort. As tempting as it may seem to apply for bankruptcy to clear all your debt and remove financial pressure from you, you will lose everything except your personal basic possessions. Don't be tempted to see this as a quick fix – ensure that you have considered every other possible solution before you file. Everything of value will be sold; this includes antiques and jewellery that you may hold dear. The bankruptcy order will include restrictions and, like an IVA, will remain on your credit file for six years from the date of the order, even though the order will be discharged after a year. Bankruptcy is a serious step and you should take advice before pursuing this option.

Pensions

One of the biggest financial mistakes that women make on divorce is not considering pensions. If you are a woman who has had a long career, you may have a very good pension. If, however, you've taken a career break or worked part time or you have worked in a lower paying job because childcare was your priority, you may have little, or no, pension. The pension is an important part of your long-term future. Looking at the income needs of both of you, your pensions will be crucial.

I often work with women who will initially tell me that they are happy for their husbands to keep their pension so long as they can have a family home. They think that this is a sensible and fair trade. Often it is not. Remember what I said above, that the house that you are living in is not just an asset, but a liability as well. You need to maintain and run it. It's also more of a liability if it's in negative equity. That might not be a concern now, but if you don't have any pension provision of your own, how are you going to manage in your old age? It might be that you're young enough to begin to build up your own pension provision, but it's also likely that you're not. Hopefully the capital asset in your home will grow, but it may not. Remember that you are statistically likely to live longer than a man, and therefore you're likely to need more money.

Sharing your husband's pension may be a sensible option for you. This will mean that when you get to a pensionable age, you will have your own source of income. A pension is a tax efficient way of saving for your retirement. If you share your husband's pension, the part that you share becomes yours. Remember that without this, you'll be living off basic state pension, which isn't very much.

Once you retire, you are able to take a 25% tax-free lump sum from your pension (under current rules). You may use this to pay off the remainder of your mortgage if you have one. Until recently, you were obliged to buy what was known as an annuity with the remainder of the fund which would give you the income for the rest of your life or you could use unsecured income drawdown.

Defined benefit pensions

Defined benefit pensions are often known as primary final salary pension schemes. These include public sector pensions, police and the armed forces. These pay out a determined undefined income at retirement. These schemes make the majority of their money in the final few years of the scheme. The transfer value of these pensions is often wholly unrepresentative of their future value. Whilst an actuarial report may be an additional expense that you'd like to avoid, it may be the best money that you ever spend. You can seek guidance from your lawyer about whether they believe this would be useful for you.

Some pensions such as those offered by the MOD (and others) have special rules attached to them in relation to how they may be dealt with on divorce. If you feel that this may apply to you, you need to take independent financial advice.

Defined contribution or money purchase pensions

Generally speaking (I'm not a pensions expert), defined contribution or money purchase pensions include those occupational or employer-sponsored pension schemes that are not final salary schemes. Money is placed into the schemes without any guarantee of the return at retirement. There are a number of different ways in which these may be invested which are beyond the scope of this book. You will need to obtain advice about how these pensions can be split and an independent financial advisor will be able to do forecasting for you.

Flexi Income Drawdown

Since 6 April 2015, those with defined contribution pensions have been able to take the whole of their pension out when they reach 55 years old. This is known as Flexi Income Drawdown. Flexi Income Drawdown allows the pension holder to take a lump sum of up to 25% out of the pension tax free without proving any secure income means. Further drawdowns can be made which are taxed at the policy holder's marginal rate. You need to be aware of this because it may mean that your husband takes his pension before you're able to share it.

UFPLS

The Uncrystallised Funds Pension Lump Sum was also brought in on 6 April 2015. An alternative to the purchase of an annuity, uncrystallised funds (those not in payment) can be taken in one or more lump sums, the first 25% of each being tax free. These only apply to defined contribution benefits and can be taken from the age of 55 years.

It may now therefore be possible for your husband's pension to be taken as cash, but there are complex rules around this, and it isn't available for everyone. Your lawyer will not be able to give you advice about this, only the most broad overview. It is a criminal offence for anyone to offer financial advice without proper qualifications and therefore you will need to seek proper independent financial advice about your particular circumstances. This information has been provided purely for you to be aware of the situation.

Pension sharing

Pension sharing is just that. You share your husband's pension (or he shares yours). Pension sharing is currently the most popular way of dealing with pensions on divorce, and allows for equality particularly if one of you has a larger pension than the other. However, calculating the amount of pension you should share depends upon its purpose. Do you want to share the pension for equality of income, or for capital purposes? Calculating equality of income on retirement means that you will likely need a larger share of the pension, because statistically you are likely to live longer. The current value, therefore, is not as important as its future value. Pension sharing does however give you control over the pension fund in most cases (there are exceptions such as MOD pensions, as I have already mentioned). This method of dealing with pension also allows for a clean break. What was once his is now yours.

Earmarking

Less common these days is the concept of earmarking. Earmarking is where a portion of your husband's pension is 'earmarked' for you, both in terms of lump sum and income. The problem with earmarking is that your husband could determine when you receive the pension. You are not able to receive a pension until it is in payment to him, and therefore he can just keep working to prevent you from receiving payment. Also, if he died before the pension became payable you would receive nothing. Earmarking has therefore fallen from favour.

Offsetting

Offsetting is where one of you takes the greater share of the assets by forfeiting your right to something else. For example, you take a larger share of the marital home and your husband keeps the whole of his pension. Your husband may be keen for this to happen, particularly if he is in a final salary pension scheme. Be cautious of this, and do not agree until you have taken independent financial advice. As mentioned earlier, you may need the support of an actuary to calculate the true value of any pension. An actuarial report will calculate the true value and will help you assess whether offsetting is appropriate for you based on its true value. Remember in the longer term the pension will grow but your house will cost you money and will only provide you with a future income when it is sold.

Post-divorce income and expenditure

Getting clear about your current income is powerful because it's easy to forget just exactly what you have coming in. If you're working, you have your salary. If you have children, you may be in receipt of Child Benefit. You may also have Child Tax Credit and/or Working Tax Credit. You may get support with Housing Benefit and Council Tax Benefit.

 Action Point

Write all these numbers down. It could be, however, that you receive an allowance from your husband, your parents or from a Trust Fund. Again, you need to write these figures down, because your husband will be expecting to see them on your Form E. This exercise is just like the assets and liabilities exercise above; it is separate, but just as important.

When you add these figures up, does it surprise you? Is that in a positive or negative way? This exercise may bring up a lot of emotion for you; remember that this is completely normal. Congratulate yourself on being willing to keep going and to face the situation head-on. Whilst it may feel really painful now, you are giving yourself the best opportunity to move forward, prepared and in control (to the extent that you can be) of the process. Remember, also, that having this information gives you the option to begin making changes, even if you do not anticipate divorcing immediately. This might be looking at a better paid job, or even getting a job if you've been a stay-at-home mother for a number of years. It may mean that you begin to consider your spending habits. Are you overspending based on your income? More importantly, perhaps, what is driving your overspending? Is it need? Is there a genuine gap between your income and your outgoings just to survive? Or are you emotionally spending to cover up unhappiness in your relationship? Take some time to consider what is true for you.

 Action Point

» If overspending is an issue for you, write down the cause. How can you reduce your overspending and/or increase your income?
» If your overspending is emotionally driven, notice what triggers it. Stress? Anger? Sadness? What can you do differently to soothe yourself rather than spending money?

Calculating future income needs

It is advisable that you get expert help in respect of calculating your future income needs. You need to understand your own attitude to risk, as well as issues such as inflation, taxation and the overall performance of the stock market so you can understand the nature of investment return. You need to ensure that you do not run out of money in the future, or before you are able to support yourself.

Financial experts use software to help them with these predictions and to show you various scenarios. This will give you the greatest insight into how your financial future may be. By working out these various scenarios, your attitude to risk, and your taxation liability, a financial advisor and your lawyer will be able to work out exactly what you need by way of a lump sum in order to provide you with that income. This can also be used in respect of calculating how much of your husband's pension you would require in order to meet that need.

What are my outgoings?

Working out your outgoings will help you feel more confident that you are calculating your future income needs correctly. Unless you are already the type of lady who has a good grasp of her spending habits, it's very unlikely that you know just how much you spend and on what. You might well say "I know that I spend everything that I earn, and maybe a little bit more!" But do you really know exactly where that money goes? You see, you can bet your husband's lawyer will scrutinise everything that you spend. From your daily latte to a cheeky little glass of wine after work, your hair appointments, nails, that magazine you picked up in Waitrose; they all add up.

 Action Point

Use your notebook to start writing down absolutely everything that you spend. Carry that notebook around in your handbag and if you can't write things down as you buy them, make a habit of doing this at the end of every day. There are also smartphone apps that you can use to make this easier. Cross check these figures with your bank statements. Remember to include the odd pint of milk, the few pounds that you give to the children, the school trip that you just paid for. Remember also to include those items that perhaps you don't pay for monthly. It could be that you have a quarterly subscription to your favourite magazine, so make sure that you include everything.

Future outgoings

Depending on how financially savvy you already are, you may have an idea about your future outgoings, and whether your current lifestyle will be maintainable. This exercise can be very painful, I understand that, but it's really important that you stick with it. Depending upon the assets of the marriage, you may be able to maintain your existing standard of living, but you may need to cut your cloth according to your means.

You need to have some kind of idea about what your future outgoings will be in various scenarios. Will you be able to take over the mortgage payments for example? Will the former matrimonial home be sold, giving you the deposit for a smaller property? Or will you be looking at rented accommodation? Begin to explore all these possibilities. As I said, some of you will have a better idea about which of these options is most likely, and which you can rule out altogether. Understanding where you are likely to be will help you emotionally to come to terms with the situation rather than having a surprise later on.

 *Action Point*

Begin to consider, if you need to, how you can reduce your spending so that you know what the absolute bottom line is for you. You do not need to share that list with your husband's lawyer. If you are in a position to get a mortgage, start making enquiries as to how much you might be able to borrow. Does that mean that you can buy your husband out? Will you be able to buy a small property? Do you know how much rental properties cost in your local area? Remember that you may need to compromise on lifestyle but that the clearer you can be about what you need and why, the more likely it is that your needs will be met.

Tax liability

Depending upon how and when you split your assets on divorce, you may be subject to a tax liability. It's vitally important that you get advice on the tax efficiency of your proposed settlement before you ask the court for a consent order. Failure to do this can be a very costly mistake. The tax implications may have an immediate or long-term impact upon your lifestyle.

You may have to pay Capital Gains Tax if you sell an asset or if it is transferred. This can include the marital home. It can include shares, trusts, investments and overseas property if you have one, or more. As married couples are allowed to transfer assets between one another tax free, you can transfer assets within the tax year of your separation but may be liable for CGT after that point.

Divorce may also have Inheritance Tax implications for you so it is important that you seek legal and financial advice before any consent orders are applied for.

Financial orders on divorce

A brief word about the range of financial remedies that are available on divorce. As this book is not intended to be a definitive guide, you may wish to seek legal advice, but this section will give you an overview of the types of order that can be agreed or made.

Maintenance pending suit

Maintenance pending suit is an application to the court for maintenance prior to the divorce being finalised. This can be used when a spouse has been denied access to finances by the other spouse.

Lump sum order

Speaks for itself: one spouse agrees or is ordered to transfer a lump sum to the other spouse.

Periodical payments order (spousal maintenance)

Either spouse may be ordered to make periodical payments. This is used in situations such as one spouse has given up work to look after the children and is no longer working. Case law now indicates that these periodical payments won't be ongoing if the spouse receiving such payments is able to generate an income. It depends on many facts and varies from case to case.

Property adjustment order

The court has power to alter the shares each spouse holds in a property, including ordering one spouse to transfer the property to the other. The court may also force sale or delay the sale of property until the children are older.

Child maintenance

The court does not have power to order child maintenance. If the two of you cannot agree the sum payable, it must be dealt with through the Child Maintenance Service, https://childmaintenanceservice.direct.gov.uk/public/. There is a fee that both you and your husband pay for using the service so, if you can, reach agreement between you.

If you are able to agree the terms of your child maintenance, you can ask the court to write this into the consent order.

How to avoid financial mistakes

Being organised about and understanding the whole divorce procedure is the key to avoiding making financial mistakes on divorce. It's important that you think strategically and logically and that you keep emotion out of your decision-making as much as possible. Will this always be easy? No. That's why hiring the services of a coach can help support you to keep your decisions practical, and your emotions in check. A good lawyer will also help by reminding you of the costs of challenging the smallest of issues and delay tactics.

This is where being organised comes into its own. Being organised means that you can keep going even though you may be experiencing extreme emotions. Your head rather than your heart needs to be in control at this time. The decisions that you make now may affect you for the rest of your life. Whilst that may sound dramatic, it's true for many women. Make a mistake, and it's very difficult, and sometimes impossible, to undo. When you understand how the divorce process works, when you are organised and you understand your financial position, you set yourself up to be in the best possible place to make a great decision.

The most expensive lawyer that you can afford will not necessarily be a good investment. A good lawyer does not have to cost the earth. Find a lawyer that shares your values. Shop around and take recommendations. Remember that if you hire a city centre lawyer with swanky offices, it will cost you more than the lawyer with lower overheads!

Be open to alternative dispute resolution such as the family mediation and the collaborative law we mentioned earlier as this may save you thousands.

Your lawyer or mediator may well recommend using other professionals to assist you. Before you write this off as an additional and unnecessary expense, remember that your lawyer is not qualified to give you independent financial advice, nor are they pension experts. It's also important that you understand the impact of taxation upon your assets; this is why the support of a specialist will help you in making the right financial decisions in the most tax efficient way for you.

Constantly phoning your lawyer for emotional support is a waste of your money. Your lawyer is not qualified to give you such support and will be billing you.

Getting caught up with the minutiae of your assets and liabilities can be a red herring which is incredibly expensive. It's important that you keep your eye on the bigger picture. This is where having the support of an independent third party to keep you straight can be extremely helpful. There may be something of great emotional importance for you, but the overall financial impact may be minimal. This can cost you a lot of money for little to no gain.

It's important that you understand your true outgoings. Failing to be open and honest about your actual needs may mean that you are woefully underprovided for.

Just as it is important that you understand your assets, it's also important that you understand the liabilities of your marriage. Remember that if you have joint debt, you are both jointly liable for the whole amount, irrespective of who spent the money and for what. It is important that the joint debt is paid prior to the conclusion of your divorce or you could be left liable for the debt if your husband defaults.

One of the biggest mistakes that women make on divorce in respect of their finances is making quick decisions to 'get it over with'. Often this is characterised by an agreement for a 50–50 split of the assets. Now I'm not saying that this is never appropriate, but you do need to take financial and legal advice about this.

Much will depend on your individual circumstances. If, for example, you have taken a career break to raise family, it may be difficult if not impossible for you to have an equal earning capacity to your husband. In respect of his pension, splitting the pot 50–50 will not necessarily give you an equal income because statistically, you are going to live longer than him. Therefore splitting assets 50–50 may mean that you are at a financial disadvantage.

Another huge mistake that ladies may make on divorce is becoming obsessed with keeping the family home. The home that you living in is an asset which hopefully will capitally appreciate (grow in value). I know I've mentioned this before, but it's crucial to remember that whilst you are living in it, your home is also a liability in that it must be maintained. It is not an income generating asset unless you are renting out a room. It's important that you consider the running costs on a day-to-day basis, and also the long-term maintenance of the property. You may find that in the short to medium term you have to sell it anyway because you can't afford to run and maintain it. This may be a very difficult decision to make, but making it now may save you even more heartache later on.

Remember too, that if you have a mortgage on your property that you are responsible for, you must factor in an increase in the interest rates over time and your ability to meet these higher costs.

Following on from this is the issue of offsetting. We have already looked at offsetting in the pension section but here's a reminder: one of the biggest mistakes is taking a larger share of an asset (usually the family home) on the basis that your husband keeps his pension, but you also need to consider how you will finance your retirement. This will depend upon your age and your circumstances, but if you get to retirement and you don't have a pension, and all you have is the former matrimonial home, you will end up selling it, downsizing potentially quite significantly, and living off the remainder. But this will be liquid cash and you will not have had the benefit of being able to invest that money to provide you with a greater return.

It's also important that you understand the liquidity of the assets that you are seeking. Remember that if you are taking a share of your husband's pension, you will not be able to access this money immediately unless you are already of pensionable age. If you are in need of cash now, it may be more appropriate that you take less pension in favour of the house or some other asset. Your lawyer and financial advisor are the best people to give you support around this.

One of the biggest challenges for divorcing women is thinking in the longer term because even when divorce is your idea it's tempting just to think about now, and the immediate future. By understanding your own values, dreams and life plan, it will be easier to design the future that you want, post-divorce. If you wait until after your divorce and financial remedy order are finalised, it may be too late. Tax, inflation, the stock market and political instability can all play a role in what the return is on your investments. You need to understand the risks associated with this in conjunction with understanding your needs and your attitudes to risk. A financial advisor is crucial to help with this.

It's also advisable to take out insurance policies on your husband's life and on the maintenance that he pays you for the children and yourself, if you have it. You may use some of the money that he pays you to pay for this policy, and if you manage the policy, you can be sure that the premiums are paid. Whilst this may feel like a luxury, particularly if cash is tight, it will protect you and your income should anything happen to your husband post-divorce.

It's important to remember that it is unlikely that you will be able to rely on spousal maintenance for the rest of your life. Once upon a time, spousal maintenance was the norm. This was because women didn't work once they got married and had a family. It was often difficult for women to find employment and be able to support themselves post-divorce. However, the world has changed and the court's attitude to spousal maintenance has moved on. Recent case law suggests that the average woman ought to expect to return to work once her youngest child is in year six (or thereabouts). You and your husband are of course free to agree otherwise, but in the absence of such agreement, the court will expect that you find employment. You may well be given spousal maintenance for a short period of time to allow yourself the opportunity to retrain for a career, or until your youngest child is in full-time school and settled. For most women, a divorce settlement is no longer a financial plan.

Section 5

Children

Introduction

Let's talk about the children.

Children and divorce is a hugely emotive topic. More so than money. Money is just money, and yes, whilst it's important, if you are a lady with children you may be feeling overwhelmed by the thought of the potential impact of divorce on your children.

Firstly, just relax.

Remember to keep perspective. In this section, we'll be considering how best to support your children, from letting them know that you're separating, to supporting them through a parent leaving the family home, your children moving to a new home or school, arrangements for spending time with each parent and when to get additional support.

Children don't have to suffer in divorce. It doesn't have to negatively impact them, and it doesn't mean that they will go on to be divorced themselves. Will your divorce be challenging and stressful for your children? Yes, of course. That can't be avoided. But if you and your husband have been arguing, or there has been tension in the air, this will cause more suffering to your children than a well-handled separation. If you want your children to have healthy adult relationships, sometimes the only way that you can do this is by showing them that it is okay to leave an unhealthy one. You see, by divorcing, you allow your children to experience that settling for what you have isn't the only option. From courage, to boundary setting, you show them that their self-esteem is their responsibility and it's okay to make decisions that make them happy.

Does this mean that they won't struggle? No. It's likely that, just like you, your children will struggle at some point through your divorce, and after.

Your child

All children are different. If you have more than one child, you may be concerned about each of their responses to your divorce. Age, gender, emotional and intellectual maturity will each have a bearing on how well your children deal with your divorce.

It's impossible to write about every child in the scope of this book. However, what all children need regardless of their age, gender, emotional and intellectual maturity, is love, certainty, boundaries and good role models. It may seem obvious, so why would I write about this? You're a parent, right? Well, here's the thing: it's so easy to lose sight of these facts when you yourself are struggling with the emotional and practical aspects of divorce. It's not because you want to; it's because you get caught up in the emotional pain of the situation. You can become defensive, and lose focus by blaming, accusing and responding to negativity. Your children get caught up in the crossfire but you're so engaged in the battle that you fail to notice. If this is already happening to you, forgive yourself, and plan now to do it differently in future.

 Action Point

How can you support yourself emotionally and avoid responding to your husband with negative emotions?

Many people avoid divorce because they believe it has a negative impact on children. Statistically, children of divorced parents are more likely to:

» do less well in school
» have low self-esteem
» become involved in underage sex, drinking and/or drugs
» get divorced themselves

But what if you would take responsibility for the emotional health of your children and do your divorce differently? Children of unhappy parents suffer. Because our children learn from us. They learn about self-esteem, boundaries and emotional security from what they see, feel and hear around them. Remove the fighting, arguing and unhappiness; create calm and stability in a loving environment, even if that's in two separate houses, and your children can thrive.

What happens to children when you don't divorce?

Children need emotionally stable caregivers. Physical comfort is not enough. When you are unhappy, your children are unhappy, even when they don't voice it, or they are too young to intellectualise it. Unconsciously, your child is absorbing everything that's going on around them. 'Making the best of it' for the sake of your children is likely to increase their feelings of insecurity and anxiety. In younger children, this can lead to separation anxiety, meaning that when one parent does finally leave, their world becomes even more uncertain.

Stay together, however, and you show your children a pattern of relationships that they are likely to repeat. They learn that unhappy relationships are normal, that it's okay to be unhappy. That point scoring, belittling and anger are the ingredients that make up adult relationships. Meanwhile, as they lie in bed listening to you argue, they're fantasising of a family that is harmonious. However, if they haven't seen it or experienced it for themselves, it becomes almost impossible for them to create in their own adult lives.

So how do you make divorce easier for your children? You make it child centred.

Child-centred divorce

The first step to making your divorce child centred, is consider your children in all your conversations with yourself, and also with your husband.

Putting your children first is beneficial in a number of ways. Firstly, it's natural that your children should be your first priority. Emotionally and practically you both want what's best for them, even if you disagree about what that is. Secondly, should you need to resort to a court making a decision, it is the 'best interests' of your children that will be the court's paramount consideration. Thirdly, by putting your children first, you can take an emotional step back from your divorce. By doing this, you give yourself the best opportunity to move forward because you're not focusing on you, your hurt, anger and disappointment. The more you focus on that, the longer and more challenging your divorce will be.

Keeping child focused supports you to recognise when you are being dragged into drama that's about you and your husband. Even if, on the face of it, you are talking about future arrangements for the children, such as where they will live and the arrangements for spending time with the other parent, it's easy to base those conversations on past resentments, hurt and anger. These conversations are not based on what's best for your children; they're based on your emotional state.

Sometimes, it really isn't in the children's best interest to have any contact with their other parent. But these situations are extremely rare. Even if spending time with their other parent has to be 'supported' or 'supervised', the courts making an order for 'no contact' is very unusual. If you are in this situation, it's highly likely that there will be significant social work involvement with your family already. The fact that your husband may be unreliable, dishonest and an inexperienced parent will not be a reason that he will automatically be denied all contact with your children.

Child-centred divorce isn't easy. It requires effort and awareness. The emotional and psychological effects of divorce on children can last for years. Many of my clients tell me that they want to avoid the destructive pattern of divorce suffered by their husbands as children. Indeed, many of them cite their husband's inability to deal with past emotional trauma as a significant contributory factor in the breakdown of their marriage. In short, if you want your children to go on to have happy marriages, it's important that you divorce in a child-centred way. Child-centred divorce means that your children recognise that your divorce is separate from them and who they are.

Telling your children that you're leaving

Telling your children that you and their father are separating is probably one of the most difficult parts of the divorce process. But do you know what? In my experience of working with women in this position, the thought of it is actually far worse than the reality. You see, your children are far smarter than you think. Depending on their age, they may well have been thinking about your separation before you were! When it happens, it may come as a shock to them, but often it's not a surprise. The shock comes from them thinking that it wouldn't happen, not that it isn't the best or right thing for you. There is a difference. A big difference. Of course, your child may not have seen your separation coming, or you may have a number of children of very different ages and different intellectual and emotional capacity. What should you do in that situation?

The strategy that I share with my clients is this. Before you even consider telling the children, discuss with your husband what, how and when you will tell the children of your impending separation. In order for your children to feel secure, they need to know what is happening now, and what will happen next. They will cope better if they see that you are on the same page, even if, in reality, you're not. Even if one of you doesn't want the marriage to end. It supports your children to know that the decision has been made, and your marriage is over. Any doubts that the children observe in you will transfer to them. This can lead to the children feeling insecure or failing to accept the reality of the situation.

 *Action Point*

Agree how, when and where you will tell the children of your impending separation and agree in advance what you will say.

If it's safe for you, it will be helpful if you and your husband can sit and tell the children together. This helps your children see that you are united in your decision. It allows them to ask questions of both of you at the same time. Now this will be dependent on their ages, but it's likely that the older children will have questions, so be prepared to answer them. If one of you is going to move out, say so. Say what will happen and when. Tell them where their other parent will be living, and when they will see them next.

 *Action Point*

» Read Angela's story next. Notice how you relate to some of the fears that both Angela and Michael had about the impact of divorce upon their daughter.

» Now your children may not react exactly the same way, but think about the ways in which you can prepare your children in the broadest sense. They'll often have many questions for you. What are they likely to want to know first? Have these answers ready for them.

Angela

One of Angela's biggest fears of divorce was the impact upon her young daughter. Michael kept telling Angela that divorce would damage her. This made Angela fearful and guilt ridden, and it prevented her from making a decision.

I asked Angela what advice she would give her daughter if her daughter felt the same way she did in her own marriage. It was a lightbulb moment for Angela. Immediately she answered that she would advise her daughter to leave. Finally, Angela had the clarity that she had been searching for.

Angela and I explored how she and Michael could prepare their daughter for their separation and ultimate divorce. We reframed the notion that it would automatically be a negative experience for her and looked at the possibility that it would be an opportunity for both her and Michael to show their daughter it's possible to leave a relationship that isn't working in a calm, kind, and dignified way and that it's okay to leave when you are unhappy.

When Angela and Michael sat down to tell their daughter that they would be separating and that she would have two homes, which meant two bedrooms, she was excited!

Where possible, tell all your children at the same time, in the most age-appropriate way for the youngest child. This allows even the smallest of your children to feel included and not feel that adult conversations are going on without them. Of course, older children will have more questions than younger ones and you can speak in a more age-appropriate way with your older children once the younger ones are elsewhere. It's likely that your younger children will soon go off to play, giving you time to chat with your older children.

Remember that your children need to hear that your separation is not about them, their behaviour or their school grades. Equally, be mindful of being age and privacy appropriate about why your marriage is ending. Unless your children are already aware of the reason, you do not need to share this with them at this time.

Remember that if you are struggling to deal with the reasons for your breakup it's important that you seek support for yourself – it isn't the role of your children to do this.

Keep the dialogue open

Telling the children that you're separating is not a one-off event. It's important that you keep dialogue open with them. Younger children can make up fantastic stories about why events are happening and make them centred around themselves. If your children don't want to talk with you, is there someone else that they would feel comfortable talking to? Grandparents, aunts and uncles, parents of school friends or teachers? Regularly check in with your children, and always be open and honest in an age-appropriate way. If you feel information they asked for is inappropriate, say so. If you don't know the answer to a question, tell them that you don't know the answer, and that you'll let them know when you do. Don't be tempted to tell lies or make promises that you cannot keep. Your children need to be able to trust you. They don't, however, need to know things that are nothing to do with them, and it's okay to let them know this. You are entitled to your privacy, and your children are entitled to be children.

 Action Point

» Read how Katie experienced separation and telling her children about divorce.
» Consider your own children if you have more than one. How do their levels of resilience differ?
» What support will each of them need?
» If you can, discuss this with your husband in advance and make it part of your Parenting Plan (see Parenting Plans) for more details.

Katie

Katie has a toddler, pre-teen and a teenager. Katie has felt much sadness that her youngest child will have no memory of living with her mother in the family home, but she was also grateful that her toddler wouldn't experience the same sadness that the older children did. I reminded Katie that her toddler, though very young, will also be experiencing the unhappy atmosphere in the family home.

Katie's older children were aware that their parents had been in marriage counselling for some time. The pre-teen in particular was preoccupied with the state of their parent's marriage and was typically fearful of the 'D' word. The older child took a much more pragmatic view.

Like Angela, Katie was concerned about how the children would cope with her moving out of the family home (she knew that Will would not). She was concerned about how the children would settle having two homes. Katie was also concerned that Will, who was angry, would not be able to give and maintain a united message to the children about the separation.

Katie and I explored these concerns which were clearly important to her. We focused on the longer term consequences of Katie and Will remaining married upon the children who were witnessing and experiencing arguments, negative comments and bullying. Katie said that she didn't want the children to think that relationships like this were 'normal'. This gave Katie the strength to leave.

Katie explored the resilience of children generally, and we also looked at the possibility that her pre-teen may need some counselling. We devised strategies for keeping connection and dialogue open with the children and for supporting their transition into being a two-home family.

Your co-parenting relationship

Your co-parenting relationship is crucial for the ability of your children to move through your divorce with their self-esteem intact. In the first throes of relationship breakdown, it's common to want to stop communication between you and your husband; you only want to communicate through texts, lawyers and, worse still, your children. This is a recipe for disaster. Now, if you are experiencing abuse, this might be appropriate. But if this isn't your situation, work on this not becoming a habit.

Is co-parenting easy? No. It will test every fibre of your being and require all your determination to put your children first. Get it right, and your children will thank you, respect and admire you for the rest of their lives. Co-parenting doesn't mean that you have to agree with each other. It doesn't mean that you can't have slightly different rules and approaches to parenting. It does mean, however, that you work together to figure out a way to parent that works for you and your children.

Agree what your primary form of communication will be. Telephone calls are always best. Texting and email can often leave too much scope for miscommunication, particularly in the early months of separation. Where trust between you is low, telephoning to make arrangements means that the other parent can hear the tone of your voice and can ask for clarification if they don't understand something. Keep communication to a minimum if you need to.

By creating a Parenting Plan (see below), you will avoid some of the stress of communicating with your soon-to-be ex-husband.

 ## *Action Point*

Discuss how and when you will contact each other in respect of the children and/or money.

Parenting Plans

You might like to consider a Parenting Plan. A Parenting Plan is exactly as it sounds – it's a plan of how you and you husband will parent, based on your values, family life and the needs of your children. If you'd like further information, you can download a copy or apply for one free from Cafcass, by following this link www.cafcass.gov.uk/grown-ups/parenting-plan.aspx.

I'm a fan of Parenting Plans because you can design them the way you want, to fit in with your life and family. Whenever possible, begin to create your plan before you speak to your children, so that they will understand what is going to be happening to them – where there will live, where their other parent will live, when they will see their extended family and school friends, for example. This supports your children's certainty and stability.

If your children are older, you may want to get them involved with the plan. Children who have extracurricular activities, homework, play dates and the like, need to be considered as part of the plan. Remember that it is your children's right to enjoy time with both of their parents, and not your right as a parent to enjoy time with your children. This is child-centred parenting. It means that your children should not be expected to give up social activities they enjoy in order to spend time with their other parent. Avoid disrupting their activities as much as possible. Instead, get involved. If activities have to end for financial reasons, that's different, but if you intend to your children to continue with their activities, and ballet falls on 'your' Saturday and football falls on 'your' Sunday, take them to these activities, and if possible stay and watch. Be as engaged with the things that your children love as you were before your separation. If you weren't that engaged before, take this opportunity to get to know this side of your child; it'll help build a deeper bond between you. Quality time is what your children will remember, not the quantity of it.

Make your Parenting Plan as detailed as you like. It might be that you add to the Plan over time, and it's likely that as your children grow, the Plan will need to change. Build in flexibility. Remember that as time goes on, it's likely that you and your husband will begin to have your own social engagements which will impact upon the Plan. Requesting 'swaps' of weekends, overnight stays, and requests to take the children on extended holidays should be anticipated, and met with an attitude of facilitation rather than creating obstacles.

Your Plan can include details of the ground rules, duties and expectations you have of one another as parents as well as those you expect of your older children. You can make agreements about things that may not yet have happened. For example, decisions about your child's first mobile phone, ear piercing or unchaperoned trips to the cinema with friends. It may also include ground rules as to how and when the two of you will introduce new partners to your children (I cover this later, in Section 7).

Think about arrangements for any religious holidays you may follow or cultural festivals. Birthdays, Christmas, you name it, you can include whatever you wish! Consider who you wish to nominate as next of kin in an emergency, if the children's other parent is not contactable. Agree how you will communicate with one another and attend routine hospital, doctor, dental and school appointments. You can use the Parenting Plan to consider all of these issues and any more that you can think of that are right for your family!

Parenting Plans are not legally binding documents. They can be as organic as you wish. Used well, they can facilitate your family working together to reach decisions that are appropriate for all of you. You can store them online where everyone has access to them, or pin them to your fridge so your children can 'count sleeps' if they like to do this. By choosing to stick to a Parenting Plan, you, your husband and your children have certainty and you can all begin to build a new 'normal'. Parenting Plans make emotional issues far more practical. They avoid the need for endless discussions and negotiations. They also allow your children to see that you both agree on key issues.

The voice of your children in the divorce process

Family mediation

Clients in family mediation increasingly ask about their children being spoken to in the family mediation process.

It is possible for your children to be spoken to by a specially trained mediator if it is appropriate. Sometimes, hearing from your children is helpful to decisions you and your husband have to make. However, your children will only be spoken to if, and only if, you and your husband both agree, and the mediator agrees that your children should be spoken to. Most importantly, your children must want to speak to the mediator.

If your children are spoken to, they get to choose whether or not you get to hear what they say. If they tell the mediator that they do not want you to know what they have said, you won't be told. What your children do tell you is for you to consider, but it will still be your responsibility to make final decisions. Many parents try to avoid bringing their children into the mediation process, and careful consideration should be given before you embark upon it. Both you and your husband need to be open and honest with yourselves about how much weight you will give to the voice of your own children. There is little point in your children being spoken to, if one of you is going to push for an outcome that the children have explicitly said they do not want.

Your child will normally be around 10 years old or older before a mediator would think it is appropriate for them to be spoken to, however emotional maturity is the key factor. Siblings may be seen separately or together, depending on the wishes of the children themselves.

Some children will be keen to be spoken to, others less so. There must be a benefit to the child in being spoken to rather than a benefit to the parents.

Children and Cafcass

Cafcass, or the Children and Family Court Advisory and Support Service, represents the voice of children in family law matters. It is their job to ensure that the voice of your children is heard in legal proceedings and that their best interests (see below) are served. If, during your divorce, you and your husband disagree about what will happen to your children, and you have been unable to reach agreement in mediation, you may be faced with dealing with court proceedings where a decision will be made for you. (Remember that this is separate from your divorce itself which only ends your marriage. Children and financial issues are dealt with separately.)

When an application to court is made in respect of a child, the case is referred to Cafcass. Cafcass officers are specially trained to deal with families. They will initially interview both you and your husband separately by telephone prior to the first court hearing. This enables them to undertake what are known as 'safeguarding' checks. These checks are carried out with the police and the local authority to clarify whether there are any welfare concerns. A short report is placed before the court three days prior to the first hearing. In my experience, due to the volume of their work, it's sometimes the case that the report is not available for your first hearing. When this happens, your hearing will be adjourned (put off) until the report is ready. The court cannot proceed without it. If Cafcass have any concerns about the welfare of your children, these will be flagged up to the court and taken into account when any decision about your children is made. If Cafcass doesn't have any concern, their role, if any, in your matter will be minimal.

At the first effective hearing, the Cafcass officer (if present), will speak to both you and your husband separately to identify areas of agreement and disagreement. They then give their professional opinion to the court on whether they feel that their input is necessary. If there are no safeguarding issues, the court will expect you and your husband to work together to reach an agreement. You may be directed or redirected to family mediation (see Section 3) to support you. The court does not want to make decisions for you, and follows the 'no order' principle (see below).

If there are concerns about the welfare of your children, including their physical and emotional health, or the ability of either of you to appropriately parent, the court may ask Cafcass to further investigate and report back.

In the absence of these concerns, if you and your husband still cannot agree arrangements for your children, the court may ask Cafcass to prepare a 'Wishes and Feelings' report on your children. This will involve your children meeting with a Cafcass officer alone either at home or at school. They may also speak to teachers, health visitors, and social workers. They will see your children with you, and with your husband, so that they get an understanding of their wishes and feelings, and also an understanding of their home environment with each parent. Once the Cafcass officer has completed their enquiries, they report back to the court with their findings and make recommendations. The court is not bound to follow the opinions of the Cafcass officer, but it is usual.

The 'best interests of the child' principle

The Children Act 1989 was introduced to reform and consolidate family law in respect of children. One of its basic principles is that any decision concerning the welfare of the child should be made in the best interests of the child. Further, the welfare of the child is the paramount consideration – hence the need for child-centred divorce. The Children Act 1989 also brought in the notion of parental responsibility – the idea that parenting is a responsibility as well as a 'right'.

This means that decisions about the children will not be based on what you want, or what is best for you. I mentioned earlier the 'no order' principle. The 'no order' principle means:

"Where a court is considering whether or not to make one or more orders under this Act with respect to a child, it shall not make the order or any of the orders unless it considers that doing so would be better for the child than making no order at all." s1(5) Children Act 1989

This means that the court expects parents to make their own decisions. If you cannot reach your own agreements, the court will make a decision for you, based on the best interests of your children. They could be decisions that neither you nor your husband like. It is therefore better if the two of you can reach agreement, even if both of you have had to compromise.

Arrangements for children and teens

Child arrangements orders

Child arrangements orders replace the older terms of 'residence' and 'contact' which you might be familiar with. A child arrangements order decides:

» where your child lives
» when your child spends time with each parent
» when and what other types of contact, like phone calls, take place

You can, of course, agree all of these things without a child arrangements order. You can use family mediation to make these decisions if you struggle to make them alone. A child arrangements order is the last resort. Once an order is in place, it must be followed.

A breach of a child arrangements order, however minor, can be a serious matter. From imposing 'contact activities' such as parenting classes; requiring Cafcass officers to monitor a person's compliance and report back to the court; ordering curfews, electronic tagging and/or unpaid work; imposing financial compensation be paid for losses sustained by the failure to comply with an order; or changing where the child lives either immediately or on a suspended basis, and ultimately, committal to prison for contempt, there can be serious consequences for non-compliance.

Questions relating to your child's upbringing

Questions related to the upbringing of your children are dealt with either through specific issues applications or prohibited steps orders. Specific issues determine what happens to your children. For example, where they will go to school, or what faith they will be brought up in. Prohibited steps prevent a parent from taking actions such as taking the children on holiday.

Again, these are issues that the court would prefer you to resolve yourselves, and you can use family mediation to do this.

Parental responsibility

As the mother of your children, you automatically have parental responsibility. If you were married to the father of your children at the time of their birth, your husband automatically has parental responsibility as well. Your husband also acquired parental responsibility for his children if he married you after their birth. Parental responsibility can also be acquired by agreement or court order.

Teenagers

Your teenager's response to your divorce may well be complex. They may display outward anger at the parent they feel is responsible for the separation and divorce. This may be a defence mechanism because deep down they have the same fears as their younger siblings. Guilt, divided loyalties and an understanding that there may well be serious financial implications to their parents' divorce can make it particularly difficult for teenagers to cope. They may also feel embarrassed.

It may be difficult to ascertain the difference between your teenager struggling emotionally with your divorce and the 'normal' emotional struggles that your child would be facing during puberty anyway. It's also highly likely that your teenager won't be able to answer that question either. It's important that you treat your teenager as a teenager. If you're overprotective and hide things from them, they are likely to feel patronised and angry. Placing an emotional burden upon them by treating them as your friend is likely to backfire. It can often be a difficult balance.

Recognise that your teenager is moving through a period of significant change in respect of their reliance upon you as a parent. Naturally, there is a desire to move towards independence whilst still enjoying the support of a family. The thought of their parents separating can therefore be additionally confusing.

Your teenager may feel the desire to escape because they feel conflicted in their loyalties. That escapism may take the form of music, shutting themselves away in their bedroom, excessive drinking and drug use or unwanted pregnancy.

Ensure that you acknowledge your teenager and their feelings, particularly if you have younger children who are taking up much of your time both emotionally and physically. Encourage your teenager to share with you, and equally make it okay for them to speak to somebody other than you. Just as with younger children, ensure that the boundaries that your teenager had prior to separation and divorce continue. Curfews, restrictions on gaming, and rules relating to personal appearance should continue. If your teenager has responsibilities around the family home, and/or a part-time job, ensure that these remain. Do ensure, however, that older teenagers do not feel that they need to become an additional parent.

When it comes to where your teenager will live, the older they are, the more weight should be given to their point of view. If they are still in full-time education, encourage them to make a decision that makes it easier for them to continue where they are. The familiarity and their peer group will support them. Once your teenager is 16 years old, the court will be reluctant to impose any order in respect of them, recognising that children of this age can simply 'vote with their feet'. Take care not to alienate your teenager if they wish to make a decision that you do not agree with.

Support for children

Even if you feel able to support your children, sometimes your children find it easier to be more honest and open with somebody other than you. Sometimes your children will struggle to express themselves at all. Be aware that, like you, your children will mourn the loss of your marriage. They may be angry, sad, cry constantly and ask persistent questions. The closer the attachment to the parent that has moved out, the more difficult it will be for your children to cope.

Ultimately, how you handle the divorce and your own emotions will affect the children far more than the divorce itself. The biggest support that you can give to your children is to facilitate continued access to their father and to avoid showing hostility towards him. Your children want to have a relationship with him and should be allowed to love him as they loved him before your separation and divorce.

Children thrive on certainty and routine, so keep their routines as constant as possible. If there needs to be major changes in their routine because you've moved house, work to establish a new routine as quickly as possible.

If you and the children remain in your family home, invite their father to see them in the home they share with you if it is safe for you to do so, as well as ensuring the children stay in the home they share with him. Initially this will help children feel grounded and safe.

Use familiar technology to allow your children to keep in contact with you or their father. Skype and FaceTime are marvellous tools for older children to use to keep in contact with parents and the wider family.

Consider using books to help your children understand divorce. There are many books that that have been written with the aim of encouraging conversation between parents and children regarding how they feel about their parents' divorce.

Make your children's teachers aware of the changes at home and tell your children that their teacher knows. If your children's school offers counselling, your child might find this useful. Keep a watchful eye on your children's relationship with their peers. It may be that your children become angry or withdrawn. Speak with your GP if you have concerns.

Whatever the ages of your children, remember:

» Remind your children that your separation and divorce is nothing to do with them.
» Remind your children that both of you still love them.
» Talk to your children together if possible.
» Agree in advance what you will tell them.
» Let your children know what will happen to them in the immediate future.
» Don't badmouth your children's father either to them or in front of them.
» Reassure your children that it's okay for them to love both parents.
» Avoid using your children as messengers.
» Let your children's teachers know.
» Keep as much routine as possible.
» Include your children in age-appropriate decision-making.
» Avoiding using your children as confidantes.

» Avoid asking your children to take sides either directly or indirectly.

» Avoid arguing in front of your children.

» Maintain ground rules, boundaries and household chores.

Consider getting professional help, if consistently:

» Your child or teen is angry or showing signs of depression.

» Your child or teen is withdrawn or secretive.

» Your child or teen's eating habits have changed dramatically, either over or under eating.

» Your child or teen's academic performance at school has dropped.

» Your child or teen is refusing to spend any time with their other parent.

» Your child or teen has lost interest in once loved social activities, hobbies or sports.

Single parent support

Being a single parent can be challenging. No doubt that as a lady who is leaving, you have thought a great deal about how you would cope as a single parent. You may or may not have friends in this position. But it's likely that you won't have fully appreciated exactly how it feels to be a single parent because you weren't one, even if you did do most of the parenting.

Even if the end of the relationship was your decision, it doesn't make single parenting any easier. You will still have your own emotional issues to come to terms with. You will still have practical matters to deal with, as well as the emotional impact upon your children to cope with.

It's important to recognise that you don't have to cope alone. Reach out to your friends and family if you can. Talk to your girlfriends in similar positions and get their advice. Meet them for coffee and offload if you need to. Look to your husband to support you with childcare if you can.

Your children may be challenging you emotionally, practically and financially and you may feel like you're doing a rubbish job. Be kind to yourself – you're always doing the best you can. Search the Internet for local single parent support groups; you might find them useful, even if it's just for a short time. Even if it's just to boost your confidence that actually, you're doing okay.

Organisations such as Gingerbread https://gingerbread.org.uk offer support for lone parents. They can offer advice on managing emotionally, dealing with your children, advice on ensuring that you are claiming any state benefits you may be entitled to, and they can offer a confidential ear when you just need to talk.

Perhaps you are a lady who has left and your children have remained with their father. You may be finding this very difficult because there is still a stigma around a mother who has left her children. It may be that your children chose to stay with their father, and that it wasn't your choice at all. You may be feeling guilt, grief and anger. Ensure you get support with that. Single parent groups can still be there for you. If you feel you need to talk to your GP do so. Deal with any signs of depression that you may have before they take hold.

Being a single parent isn't easy. Accept that there will be times when you wish you had done things differently. Don't dwell on those; keep moving forward, doing the best you can. It will get easier. The boundaries and routines that you put in place for your children to support them will actually support you. From getting support with chores around the house, to ensuring that the children go to bed on time, leaving you with some time for yourself each evening. In order to be the best parent you can be, you need to take care of yourself first.

Children and their grandparents

Often, one of the biggest losses to children on their parents' separation or divorce is their grandparents. Often grandparents feel that they have to take sides. However, if your children have enjoyed a close relationship with your husband's family, why should that be interrupted?

If you have enjoyed a good relationship with your in-laws, why should that end? You are divorcing your husband, not his family. If you can, talk to his parents and tell them how important they are to you (if they are) and your children. Your in-laws may become an even greater source of support for you and your children now that you are divorcing. Equally, if your husband enjoyed a close relationship with your parents, encourage them to maintain that relationship with him.

Under English law, grandparents don't have the right to apply to the court if they have been refused contact with their grandchildren. They can, however, ask the court for permission to make an application. This is known as 'leave to apply'. If your children's grandparents are granted leave to apply, and they can show that their grandchildren have enjoyed regularly spending time with them and have a positive and important relationship with them, it's likely that the court will make an order allowing the children to spend time with their grandparents.

By remembering to put your children first, you'll recognise the importance of this relationship in their life even if you and your in-laws don't get on. There are many ways in which this relationship can be facilitated without your involvement.

The children of our case studies

All of the children in our case studies knew that their parents were unhappy. They are of varying ages, and have different points of view. When it comes to children and divorce, no one size fits all.

Angela and Michael's daughter was excited about having two homes.

Katie's children had mixed responses. Her youngest child was too young to understand. Her eldest child had more understanding and was frustrated and angry by Katie and Will's behaviour. Their middle child struggled most. Not only did they struggle with the 'D' word but they were also preoccupied with the notion that either parent may start to date again.

Yvonne's children recognised that change was needed. Like Angela and Katie, Yvonne was clear about keeping the dialogue open with her children and let them know in an age-appropriate way what was happening. This made transitions easier when Yvonne had left the family home. The children had bedrooms in her new home whilst maintaining bedrooms in the family home.

Section 6

Looking after yourself

Introduction

Perhaps you find it strange that a book about divorce contains a section on looking after yourself? Perhaps you think that looking after yourself is not a priority. However, I believe that self-care is the cornerstone of managing your divorce. By rights, this section should be at the front of this book, but I suspect that many of you would skip it, wanting to get to the nitty-gritty. I'm hoping that, now you are near to the end, you will be willing and open not only to reading this section, but also to implementing some of my suggestions.

Divorce takes its toll physically and emotionally, as well as financially even if it's your idea. My clients are often surprised by this because they have assumed that because divorce is their idea, because they believe it to be for the best, and because some of them are looking forward to being divorced, they assume that it will be easier for them.

It's vital that you get clear about how to look after yourself during your divorce. You see, you may feel rubbish about yourself now. You may feel worthless, unloved and your confidence might be through the floor, but the truth is, we are all responsible for ourselves, even when we are in a happy fulfilling relationship. Remember how happy and confident you felt when you were in love and you felt loved? That you is still there and worth nurturing.

When you look after yourself during your divorce, you're actually in a better place to take care of your children and manage the wider family fall-out. The biggest benefit, though, is that you invest in you. Investing in yourself builds your self-esteem; it helps quieten the negative voice in your head that's telling you that you've failed, that you're not capable of sustaining a relationship and that you've let your children down.

In my professional experience, ladies who leave experience similar physical and emotional effects to those ladies who have been left. It is therefore important that you make looking after yourself a priority. Whilst you may feel that you need to attend to the needs of your children and wider family, putting yourself first is the sensible thing to do. You see, if you don't cope, those around you will also struggle. Remember how the air steward reminds us to place our own oxygen masks on first in the case of emergency? Well, your divorce is an emergency. It is first and foremost the loss of your marriage. Whilst it's true that your divorce will have an impact on others, no one else will experience it quite the way you do.

There are a number of ways in which you can look after yourself. Some of them will resonate with you and others less so. It's important that you do what is right for you, and I also encourage you to try some of the ideas perhaps less comfortable for you to see how they support you. Remember that if you have not been divorced before, you can't say for certain what will support you, so remain open.

What to do first

At first, do nothing

Reacting is one of the worst things you can do when faced with divorce. Even if it's your idea and you've been thinking about nothing else for weeks, it takes time to really land in your body once that thought has left your mouth. Thinking is one thing. Saying and doing are separate things. Let it settle with you and your husband for a while.

Acknowledge your feelings

Acknowledging your feelings can be painful. There may be a strong temptation to push them down. I understand. Perhaps you think that you don't have time for them, or that once you start feeling your emotions you'll become overwhelmed? However, the short-term fix may well cause long-term problems. Dealing with your feelings at the time you are experiencing them is easier than revisiting them in the future – and you will.

Having a healthy divorce involves dealing with the issues in your current relationship, not leaving them until you are in the middle of your next relationship, or, worse still, your trauma and upset prevent you from moving on.

Sharing with the right people

It's important that you share your feelings with the right people. Your children are not the right people to share with, neither are those who are emotionally involved – family members and even friends. As well-meaning as they are, their relationship to you makes it difficult for them to be objective in their support. Talking with a therapist or divorce coach can help you focus on what's important and on what will help you move forward without any agenda of their own.

Your lawyer is not your therapist

Remember that your lawyer is not your therapist and it's not their job to support you this way. It's a very expensive way not to get the support you need. Unless you need to discuss legal or financial issues, avoid using your lawyer to discuss your feelings. It is, however, important that you find a lawyer that understands what is important to you – it's one of the first things a good lawyer should ask.

Counselling

I talked about relationship counselling in the context of it helping you decide whether you should stay or go, but you can go to relationship counselling on your own! You can choose to use the same relationship counsellor you used with your husband, or you can find another one if you wish.

It might be that a psychotherapist would be more beneficial for you if you feel that your issues are rooted deeper than in your relationship itself. Counselling is always confidential (subject to safeguarding issues), which means that you can talk as freely as you wish.

Letting go, opening up and speaking your truth is healthy as it allows you the opportunity to heal. It also allows you to build your self-esteem, resilience and trust in you.

Be honest with yourself

Be honest with yourself about the role that you have played consciously or unconsciously in the breakdown of your marriage. Not only is it important for your future relationships that you can acknowledge behaviours you may do differently in future, but it also helps to keep perspective, to understand the hurt and anger that your husband may be feeling, and allows the divorce to proceed without getting caught up in the drama of blame. That's not to say you should blame yourself either. It's not about that. Being honest just means accepting your part. No judgement. No blame.

Communicate

Keeping the lines of communication open when you're getting divorced can be challenging. I get that. The thing is, in my experience as a family mediator and divorce coach, lack of communication is the number one reason divorce becomes messy and expensive. By talking with your husband about your divorce you can begin to move forward both in practical and emotional ways.

In communicating, you can begin to look at why you are getting divorced and, as hard as it may be, begin to take joint responsibility for the end of your marriage. The hard truth is that happy relationships don't end. There, I said it. Happy relationships don't end. It takes two people to end a relationship just as it takes two people to make one. Perhaps it's you that was unhappy; perhaps it was your husband. I'm guessing that if one of you was unhappy, then deep down you both were. Admitting this can be hard. It can be terrifying. But. And it's a big but. Do this now; accept, forgive and learn, and you can move forward without anger and resentment. In terms of divorce, anger and resentment are expensive commodities.

Recognise when you are being driven by unhelpful emotions

As humans, we are always being driven by our emotions; it's impossible not to be. However, there are times when we make decisions based on anger, fear, irrationality and the desire to cause suffering to others. We usually come to regret these decisions. This is why I share with my clients the importance of having a plan for your divorce before you start. Avoid making decisions or responding to emails, texts, telephone calls or letters when you know that you are not in a great space emotionally. Recognise that you are entitled to time and space to work things out at your own pace. If you feel pressured, say so. Remember that you can turn off your mobile phone or decide not to read emails or text messages. Not only is this self-care, but it may well save you time and money in your divorce.

Having a plan

Having a plan before you start your divorce can really assist you. It really is self-care at its best. Putting a plan together before you start means that you can refer back to it when things get tricky or you feel overwhelmed. Having a plan means that you're less likely to overreact or act out of spite (fear) or anger in the heat of the moment. Your plan becomes your emotional safety net. Having a plan and an overview of the divorce process before you start also gives you a sense of direction – knowing what will happen and when. Having certainty can support your self-care.

Uncertainty causes stress, can make you feel anxious and can also have a negative impact on your motivation to move forward. Perhaps the child inside you wants to ask "are we nearly there yet?" because you're frustrated, bored, struggling financially and angry. Create certainty where you can. It will support you emotionally and motivate you to keep moving forward.

Exercise

Exercise may be the last thing that you feel like doing. Perhaps curling up on the sofa with a bottle of wine, Bridget Jones style, is tempting, but it's not going to help. Exercise will lower your stress levels and keep your immunity strong. Physical tiredness can help you sleep when mental tiredness just keeps you awake.

When you feel like your emotions are controlling you rather than you controlling them, exercise can help. Feel angry? Use exercise as a way to vent those feelings. Boxercise, running, martial arts: do whatever takes your fancy! If you just want to go for a long walk with the dog and talk to yourself out loud (oh yes you do), then do it! The fresh air will revive you, and support you to feel calm and relaxed. Exercise will help you with depression if it's already taken hold, and will significantly reduce your chances of experiencing it otherwise.

Perhaps exercise is something that you enjoy and do regularly. Sometimes we exercise as a way of feeling in control of ourselves, particularly if everything around us feels out of control. Be conscious of your levels of exercise. Ease off if you recognise that you may over exercise as a form of self-punishment, or your need to feel in control increases. Over exercising can deplete you both physically and emotionally.

Divorce coaching

Consider using a divorce coach

You've probably heard of business coaching, career coaching and life coaching, right? Before you yawn and think big hair and blindingly white teeth; before you think 'Oh no, not another crazy one-minute wonder', divorce coaching is a well-established profession. If you've never been divorced before, you've probably never heard of it. And why would you? But here's the thing. A divorce coach can support you to make great emotional and financial decisions at a time when you aren't feeling your best.

Before you think that divorce coaching is for people who are 'weak' or 'can't cope', let me set the record straight. Divorce coaching is not like that. Divorce coaching is not counselling. Counselling is very much focused on the past, looking at what went wrong, why it went wrong, how it made you feel and why.

So, what is coaching? Coaching is a way of supporting individuals to achieve specific or personal goals. It's future and solution focused. This is very useful for many people, particularly when you're getting divorced.

A divorce coach is not your best friend or your lawyer

A divorce coach is there to support you throughout your divorce, from helping you decide on whether a divorce is what you really want, to how to go about it and how to get through it. A divorce coach will explain what your options are, and support you through emotionally. A divorce coach will not give you legal advice, even if, like me, they are legally trained. That's not the purpose of a coach. A divorce coach is there to help you decide for yourself what you want. If you need legal advice, you go to your lawyer.

Divorce coaching is designed to help you stay in control of the decisions you need to make. We can discuss the legal advice you receive and we can discuss and future pace your options. Future pacing your options means looking at the benefits and consequences of the options available and seeing how they might work out for you in the future. Your divorce coach does not sit in judgement and is not there to make decisions for you however difficult you may find those making them. What your divorce coach will do, however, is support you to make the best decisions that you can for yourself, with the information that you have.

A divorce coach is not an alternative to psychotherapy

The end of a relationship can be very tough, even if it was your idea or you at least agree that your relationship should come to an end. It's very common to feel lost and alone at this time and you may struggle with depression or anxiety. If you need the support of your GP, seek it. Whilst some divorce coaches may be trained in counselling skills like me, divorce coaching is not counselling and it is not a substitute for therapeutic intervention.

If you are being supported with medication or are using talking therapies prescribed by your GP, a divorce coach may also be very useful to support you with the practicalities and day-to-day emotional support that is required. A divorce coach is employed specifically to help you manage your divorce.

Angela on working with me

"Coaching with Emma not only gave me the inside track to divorce and the issues to consider, it also gave me insight into myself and my own needs. The Clarity Day gave me just that, and I remember this as a turning point, starting the process that enabled me to have the divorce I wanted, in the way I wanted. Thanks to Emma, there is such a thing as a 'good divorce'."

Yvonne on working with me

"The ride since I left has been a rollercoaster but I am not regretting my decision …

"Your coaching helped me make the decision to leave and it helped me understand and face up to the reality of it and gave me the wherewithal to start doing something about it.

"You also helped me believe in myself and supported me emotionally, practically and in more ways than you probably know. It was so good to have you on the end of the phone. After our session, having talked everything through with you it began to make sense. It also helped pave the way for me to feel strong enough to tell other people, which was harder than I could imagine. I didn't look back and still haven't.

"Thanks so much and I would encourage anyone else, like me, who is on the fence or who has been on the fence about their decision for years and years to talk to you!!

"I appreciate it was something I paid for but it was worth every penny!"

A divorce coach will help you get clear and support you unconditionally

Not only will a divorce coach help you get clear about your options and what you want, they also help you look at your values and what's important to you. They help you decide the things that you need to achieve both emotionally and financially in order to be secure and happy, post-divorce. They help you get organised both practically and emotionally. Because they are independent, they are not emotionally involved which means that they act only to support you in your best interests. There are no 'hidden agendas'.

So, there you have it. Now you know what a divorce coach is and what they can do for you. Divorce coaching is a smart choice during difficult times.

Taking care of yourself physically and emotionally

Watch what you eat and drink

Stress can have a negative impact physically as well as emotionally. It is therefore important that you eat well during your divorce. Ensure that you and your children eat nutritionally balanced meals and that you avoid rich carbohydrate-based meals late at night as these may impair your sleep.

Monitor your own alcohol intake. That relaxing glass of wine that takes the edge off isn't a problem unless you start relying on it. Remember that alcohol is a depressant and too much of a good thing will make you feel physically unwell and may cause you to behave in ways you would rather not.

Treat yourself

Treat yourself in accordance with your budget. Treating yourself is all about doing something that you want to do. Perhaps you like massage or sitting in the spa. Perhaps a long hot bath or lunch with friends is your thing. It doesn't really matter what it is; it's important that you take time for yourself and show yourself love.

Treating yourself should be separate from any treat that you share with the children. Treating yourself is only about you! Some of you reading this will feel uncomfortable, because it's not something that you're used to doing, but every new skill takes practice and I invite you to start practising now!

Sleep

When you decide to divorce, you may sleep better than you've done for ages because you have finally been open and honest with yourself and your husband. The pressure of feeling guilty may feel like a distant memory.

It's likely, however, even if divorce is your idea, that you'll have sleepless nights. Your bedroom is an easy place to start ruminating about all the things that went 'wrong' in your marriage, and all the challenges you have yet to face.

Perhaps you have already experienced that feeling of tiredness that draws you to bed and then bam! You're wide awake and your brain is going 100 mph. You might be tempted to use these times as an opportunity to get up and do more housework, paperwork or work on that project you have going on at work. Resist this temptation. Sleep is important. It is restorative both physically and mentally. It is during your sleep that your unconscious mind processes all your thoughts and the information that your brain has received during the day. It's likely, then, that you will be in particular need of sleep as you progress through your divorce, so make it a priority.

Prepare to give yourself the opportunity to get the best night's sleep you can. Avoid alcohol and all caffeinated drinks before bed. Turn off all mobile devices at least one hour before going to bed. If you enjoy reading, allow yourself to wind down with a good book.

Consider journaling. Journaling is perhaps just a modern phrase for writing a diary, and in recent years, it has gained popularity as a method of downloading and organising your thoughts. Seeing your thoughts on paper allows them to become 'real' in the sense that they become more than just thoughts. Seeing your thoughts in front of you allows you to consider them from a different perspective. It can be easier to evaluate whether your concerns are genuine or just made up based on your fears. Getting your thoughts out of your head can help you rest.

If you find it hard to relax, you might wish to explore using meditation or hypnosis. There are plenty of apps, YouTube videos, books and courses available to give you a taste. Meditation and hypnosis have been found to reduce stress and promote wellbeing.

Sleep will also replenish depleted hormones. Serotonin and dopamine levels rise during sleep enabling you to feel more positive. Leptin levels are also replenished, enabling you to make healthier food choices. During sleep, your cortisol levels decrease, reducing stress.

There may be times throughout your divorce where sleep evades you. Seek help from your GP if the suggestions in this section don't work for you.

Create and enforce your boundaries

Creating boundaries in your divorce might seem like an obvious step. But let me ask you this, have you taken it yet? In reality, creating boundaries in your divorce can actually be quite tricky. You see creating boundaries in your divorce means doing things differently. It means taking a stand. It means you're 'putting out there' a new way of being. This can be a struggle at first because you have to re-wire your brain so that you can create a pattern of consistent new behaviour. You also have to deal with the fall-out of the confusion of others around this, particularly your husband. It may also include his family and your friends.

So what kind of boundaries do you need to put in place? Well, there are no hard and fast rules on this, and much will depend on your individual circumstances, how your relationship was prior to separation, and where you're living will also be a factor. Here are a few things to consider; there will be plenty more.

On deciding to separate

On deciding to separate, it's important that you consider some immediate boundaries. The benefits of boundaries are:

» They keep you safe emotionally (and possibly physically too).
» They give you clarity.
» They give other people clarity about what's acceptable or not.
» They support your children to understand that even though you both love them, things are different between you and their father.
» They keep you focused.
» They allow the healing process to take place.
» They will save you time and money.

The sooner you put boundaries in place, the sooner you will be able to begin to move forward, taking the practical steps you need to do to end the marriage and also to move forward emotionally.

Moving out of the marital bed

Have you moved out of his bed yet? I'm not being nosy; it's just that this is a big one that often gets overlooked. If you are still in your husband's bed, you're not the only lady in this situation, believe me. Most of my clients, when they start working with me, tell me they are leaving, that their husband knows they are having these thoughts and yet they still get into bed with him each night. Here's why this isn't creating the boundaries that you need:

Firstly, the marital bed holds so many memories. Some won't be happy memories. You may have lain there next to your husband feeling totally isolated and alone. It's actually more difficult to be with someone who you're not connected to than to be alone, isn't it? If you haven't experienced that, you may. Other memories will be of happier times. Of closeness, intimacy and love making. Your children may have been conceived and even born in that bed. By staying there, you are giving yourself and your husband mixed messages. Even if ultimately you envisage staying in the house on your divorce, moving out of the bedroom is within your control at this time. If your husband is struggling to come to terms with the end of your relationship, allow him that space to grieve. It may well be where he feels safest. If you choose to use that room as yours once you no longer live together, redecorate it and get new bedding. If you can, move the furniture round so that it becomes 'mine' rather than 'ours'.

Moving out of the marital bed is vital once you've told your children. They need to be able to see the beginning of physical separation, even though you and your husband may continue to share the house for some time. Allowing the children to see this supports them in the transition you are all going through.

Keys to the family home

If there's one issue that pushes buttons when I'm coaching ladies who leave, it's the issue of keys to the family home, and keys to their new home. Ladies will often remark that they "don't want him coming round whenever he feels like it". My response is always this: "So you accept that you can't just turn up at his house when you feel like it?" This is often met with silence. Hmm. You see, psychologically, that 'house' is still theirs. They may currently be the legal joint owner of that place, but it's more about the feelings that that house is still their 'home'. It's painful recognising that it is not. The thought of this is often something that gets overlooked, so I invite you to consider that as soon as you are certain that you will leave. Doing this helps you to begin to detach from that space emotionally. It's often more difficult than you might imagine.

Freedom to do what you want

Is freedom to do what you want a boundary issue? In my opinion, yes, it is. When you've been in a long-term relationship, you've probably got used to running ideas past your husband. You might have even got to the place where you stopped doing things because you got feedback from him that it wasn't ok, or he wasn't around to look after the children. You just stopped doing the stuff you loved. Now you don't have to ask his opinion. His opinion is irrelevant, unless it has a direct impact on the health and wellbeing of the children. It can take time to get used to that and it may feel really weird. The boundary is that you don't have to share that information unless you want to. If he asks you, remember whether you share the information is your choice.

Action Point

Review the case studies of Angela, Katie and Yvonne. They are ladies just like you – smart, funny, loving and loyal. They understood what they needed to do but, like you, they struggled with the decision.

During our work together, there'd be times of clarity and certainty and hope and times of dread and fear and worry.

Focusing on you is an absolute must if you want to move through divorce as confidently and calmly as you can. Your children are the responsibility of you and their father, and your husband is his own responsibility.

Putting yourself first is smart because if you are coping, so will your children and those who love and care for you.

Angela, Katie and Yvonne

I've yet to work with a lady who hasn't struggled with the idea of putting themselves first when it comes to divorce. It's the thing that stops them leaving in the first place. Worrying about their husband and how he'll cope. Worrying about how the children will deal with the divorce, and worrying about how their parents will take the news!

Our ladies were no different. I reminded them that they had already put their husbands and children first by staying in their marriages as long as they had. Going to relationship counselling, telling their husbands they were unhappy and accepting that nothing had changed was perhaps evidence that they had done all they could to improve their marriages. It was now time to focus on themselves.

Each of them struggled at first. But as their confidence grew, their self-esteem began to increase and they were more accepting that in order to take care of their children, they needed to take care of themselves. That meant leaving.

It wasn't always easy. Angela and Katie were met with requests to go back to relationship counselling once their husbands realised that they were serious about divorce. We explored what would be gained from this, and what the likely outcomes would be. Both ladies thought that nothing would change and that over time, previous behaviours would re-emerge. Both said "no" to further relationship counselling. This was both painful and powerful.

All our ladies began to put their needs first. They found it useful to be reminded that taking care of themselves was also acting as a good role model to their children. Letting go of worrying about their husband wasn't easy, but at least they could relax knowing that their children had a good relationship with their fathers which is what they wanted all along.

What can you do today?

So what can you do today to start looking after yourself? Who can you turn to? What can you do differently? What ground rules or boundaries can you put in place? Remember that you are responsible for you and that you are important. You are just as important as your children, your parents and your soon-to-be ex-husband. If you struggle to remember that, try using affirmations. I spoke about affirmations in Section 1; revisit it now for a reminder.

Your friends and family

Asking for support without justification

Another area that it's useful to create boundaries around is asking for support without justification. A particular case in point is around childcare. I often work with couples in family mediation who discuss childcare arrangements. Parents discuss and make plans for the children on a weekly or monthly basis. When a parent comes and asks the other parent to 'swap' a night or weekend because of plans they have, often a parent will want to know what the event is, and will only agree to the swap if they agree with the event. For example, a parent may want a weekend to go and visit a sick parent and the other parent may agree to the 'swap' on that basis. However, if the parent wants the 'swap' because they have been invited to a friend's hen or stag weekend, the other parent disapproves and refuses. This is a form of control.

As difficult as it is, once you are separated, you don't get to judge what the other parent does unless it is damaging to your children. If a swap is asked for, you are either willing and available that weekend or you're not. The boundary issue here is important. Neither of you will move on if you attempt to exert control upon the other. This of course cuts both ways. Is it easy? No. It's not always easy. It can take practice, a lot of practice. However, by creating the boundary that you don't need to justify what you do, both of you will move forward in trusting each other. It's likely your communication will improve and both you and your children will be happier.

The opinions of others

As well as the opinion of your husband, there are also the opinions of others to consider. When friends and family want to add their thoughts into the mix whether you asked for it or not! Mostly, you will find these comments well meaning, but not always helpful. What if you have a friend or family member who disapproves of your decision? It happens. Well, when this happens, thank the person for their concern and politely ask them not to comment further. You do not have to accept their views even when it's a parent. Consider asking that person whether, notwithstanding that they disagree with you, they are willing and able to support your decision. (It's possible to support a decision you disagree with.) If they don't feel able to support that decision, decide how much time you want to spend with them right now. Be mindful of who you share with and who you don't. You don't have to tell everyone. Share with those who will support you, those who will listen and be there for you. This is your divorce; you and your husband get to do it your way.

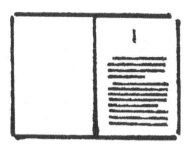

Section 7

Life after divorce

"At what point should you consider your life after divorce?" a client asked. In coaching circles, we talk about 'knowing your outcomes'. Knowing your outcome means making a decision about where you want to go before you set off.

Sometimes, when you have plenty of time, it's nice to go for a 'Sunday drive' – you know, the type of drive where distance and direction are not as important as enjoying the view. Time and destination are of no consequence.

There are other times, however, when knowing where you're going is absolutely crucial. Arriving at your destination in both a timely and relaxed manner sets you up for the day. So you plan.

You decide where you're going to go, and how you're going to get there. It's the same with divorce.

The point at which you start considering your life after divorce is of course a matter for you, but notice how much thoughts of your future life dictate your emotions around leaving. You dream of a different life. You think about the freedom emotionally and financially. You think about the possibility of another relationship where you're happy and the needs you didn't get met in this relationship are fulfilled.

There may also be times when you feel pessimistic about the future either financially or emotionally. You wonder how you will cope and whether you will actually meet another partner. At either time, you're thinking about your life after divorce.

I encourage you to start considering your life after divorce just as soon as you can. This includes a realistic assessment of your financial situation so that you can begin to transition both emotionally and physically into your life as a divorced woman. It may take you some time to come to terms with any possible change in lifestyle, and the sooner you can begin to make peace with this, the sooner you can look forward to all the positive aspects of your divorce.

It may be that you haven't started the divorce process yet – indeed you may not have decided whether divorce is what you do want, but I invite you to read this section now anyway so that you can begin to consider some of the issues that are contained within it. By knowing where you are going, it's easier for you to create a plan, take a course of action, or make decisions that will lead you to that outcome, rather than taking a reactionary stance which may lead you in the wrong direction and cause you harm emotionally and financially.

Congratulations! You have your decree absolute

As mentioned earlier, you can apply for your decree absolute six weeks and one day after the pronouncement of your decree nisi though it's unlikely that this will happen if you have financial matters to resolve. For clarity, it is possible to divorce before your financial matters are resolved, and there may be good reasons for doing this. However, you should take legal advice specific to your individual circumstances before making a decision. As with the decree nisi, you don't have to be in court for the pronouncement of the decree absolute, and you will receive a copy in the post. It's important that you put it somewhere safe, as this is the document you will need to prove that you are divorced (and should you so wish, free to marry).

How will you feel when you are finally divorced? Well, just like you, I don't know. Elation, sadness, happiness, upset, anger, numbness, relief: it could be a whole range of emotions and it may well vary from day to day and month to month, as you begin your new life as a divorced woman. Perhaps you'll expect to grieve and you don't or conversely you don't expect to and you do. If you are used to planning ahead because you have a busy work or social life, it may be worth giving yourself some space as you begin to get a sense of when you might finally be divorced so that you have some time to yourself if you need it.

The divorce itself can be quite an anticlimax. Whilst negotiations around the children or financial settlement may have had periods of tension, upset and drama, the legal ending of your marriage can feel like a bit of a non-event.

Marking the end of your marriage

Whether you choose to mark the end of your marriage or not is entirely up to you. You may have seen in the media that some people like to throw divorce parties! If you're a girl who likes to party, why not? If for you the end of your marriage is something to celebrate, then celebrate. For others, that won't feel appropriate even though divorce was your decision and you're happy with it. You may choose to mark the end of your marriage in another way, or not at all – do what you feel is right for you.

What next?

So what are you going to do next? Perhaps you have moved house, or you have the family home for yourself and the children. It may take a bit of time to get used to being divorced even though you may have been living on your own and separated for a while. Now it really is all about you (and the children if you have them); you get to choose what to do, when and how.

Housekeeping (the tedious bit)

When you petition for divorce, you will be required to send in your marriage certificate. On the pronouncing of your decree absolute, you will be issued with a certificate of decree absolute and a court number. Remember to keep these in a safe place (I know I've mentioned it before but it really is important)! These are evidence that you are divorced and will be required to show that you are free to marry if you choose to marry in the future.

Depending how long you have been separated, you may have begun to do some of the following things already. If you have, that's great. If not, work through the list at a pace that's right for you – you can remain calm and avoid feeling overwhelmed. Remember, prioritise the list according to your individual circumstances.

» Close any joint bank accounts that remain open. This may have been done on your separation, but if it hasn't, it's likely that it will be a requirement of the court order once funds have been apportioned.

» Did you know that you may be entitled to Working Families Tax Credit, Child Tax Credit or Child Benefit (if you weren't claiming)? These benefits can make a real difference to you and your children. You can find out more at www.gov.uk/browse/benefits.

» Let your children's schools know that your divorce has been finalised. Letting them know this means that they can support your children if necessary. Some schools now have counsellors to talk specifically with children whose parents are separating and divorcing.

» If you have remained in the former matrimonial home, remember to update your mortgage lender of any changes.

» If you are using a lawyer, they will remind you that you need to update your will now that you are divorced. You may of course still have your former spouse as a beneficiary, particularly if you have children together. However, your will must make it explicit that this is a post-decree bequest. Remember too that on remarriage any will that you have will be invalid.

» Are you changing your name? We'll talk about that later, but if you do, you'll need to change your passport and your driving licence. You can do this here:

https://www.gov.uk/changing-passport-information/name-divorce-deed-poll-forenames-title and https://www.gov.uk/change-name-driving-licence. Remember too to change your name on your own accounts, utility bills, at the vets, dentist and GP. It's amazing how easy it is to forget which name you're using as time goes on, so make yourself a list and tick it off as you go!

» As with your will, it's important to update the details on any insurance policies you have, particularly if these are policies that are continuing from your marriage to provide protection for you and your children.

» Remember to notify Her Majesty's Revenue & Customs of your new situation and contact details if they change: www.gov.uk/tell-hmrc-change-of-details/change-name-or-address. This will include letting them know if you have resigned from any formal role within your husband's business.

I know it's really boring but it has to be done! Notice how you feel about it. Does it motivate and inspire you or are you dragging your heels a bit? Neither is good or bad, by the way; it's just that you might find it a useful way of checking in with yourself and how you really feel.

Personally, I'm a list maker and I like to buy list making notebooks which are long and thin (similar to the one your mum had for her shopping), and they're oh so pretty … but I digress. Make your list at the start of your divorce; that way you can tackle it as you go along, a bit at a time. It's so therapeutic crossing things off as you go!

Managing your money

For some, managing your money after divorce will be no different – you were the money manager in the relationship. Perhaps you ran a tight ship, and knew exactly what was coming in and going out each month. You managed all the bills, took care of the pets and children and organised holidays, parties and gift giving. You might be the Queen of the Spreadsheet or have your own unique system, it doesn't matter; you feel confident that the management side of your money will be ok. Whether there will be as much as you'd hoped might be a different issue, but you're used to budgeting and savvy at finding out the best ways to get value for money, save cash and somehow make ends meet. If you have a lump sum to invest, you know exactly how to get the best return for your investment and you're determined to rebuild your financial life.

For others, it might be that you're managing your money for the first time in a long time and it can be really scary, confusing and overwhelming. Perhaps your husband dealt with all the finances – paid all the bills, mortgage, sorted out the tax and insurance on your car, set up life policies and invested spare cash in plans you know little about. If this is you, just breathe.

Remember, by the time you get to this stage in your divorce, you will have undergone disclosure and will have a clearer understanding of what you want, need and have now received. Use this time now to stay on top of your finances. Create a 'budget' if you need to. I don't necessarily mean you have to be careful of what you spend (and you may need to), but even if you don't, tracking where you spend your money helps you to make smarter decisions going forward.

My good friend Julie The Money Coach (www.juliethemoneycoach. com) taught me to 'pay myself first'. Paying yourself first is about putting money aside in an account for the future first – before you do anything else. Treat it as a bill you have to pay – you, first! Ideally this should be 10–12% of your net monthly income. So how do you work out what you can afford?

Firstly, you need to know what monthly (income) you have from all sources. Include maintenance for you (if you receive it), the children's maintenance, Child Benefit, any Tax Credits as well as any salary or wages you earn.

Next, calculate your expenses. Some of these will be fixed (the same every month) and some will be variable (change each month). These will include rent/mortgage, utilities, groceries, travel etc. Have an emergency fund of 3x your monthly expenses.

Once you know what your expenses are, you can minus them from your income. The rest is yours. You can choose to pay yourself the remainder or a percentage of it. If there isn't any remainder, what steps can you take to increase your income and/or reduce your expenses? Are you on the best deals for utilities, mobile phones and car insurance? It pays to shop around annually and ask for discounts. If you can't put 10–12% away each month, put away what you can. Have an account where you put cash aside for gifts, holidays and annual expenses. Paying yourself first in this way means you can relax, knowing that money is there if you need it.

If you have large sums to invest, ensure that you get good financial advice if you haven't already. Good financial planning will ensure that you have income to live on in the most tax efficient way.

What's in a name?

Some ladies revert to their maiden name on divorce; others pick a completely new name and others stick with their married name – the choice is yours. It's personal preference. Considerations will include whether you want to dissociate from your husband completely, the needs and views of any children and whether it actually matters to you – and it might not.

If you decide to change your name by reverting back to your maiden name, your decree absolute, marriage certificate and birth certificate will be evidence of your intention when accompanied by a signed statement to that effect. You will need to apply to the court for the return of your marriage certificate.

If you decide to change your name to something else, you can do this by Deed Poll. You must sign to say that you abandon the use of your previous surname, that you will use your new name at all times, you will require everyone to address you by your new name and you must sign the declaration in your old and new names. There are a number of online agencies that can help you with this.

If you want to change the surname of your children, the situation is more complex. If your ex-husband holds parental responsibility for your children he must give his written consent. It may be advisable to talk to your lawyer about this as your former husband may issue court proceedings to prevent you from doing this.

Relationships past, present and future

Your relationship with your former husband

It's important that your relationship with your now ex-husband has clear boundaries. Using mediation can be a great venue for discussing how you will be with each other. It may even form part of the Parenting Plan if you make one. You can have clear boundaries over telephone calls, text messages, visits to the house, arrangements for the children, the payment of maintenance, holidays, whatever you feel is appropriate. If you can have this resolved before you get divorced, so much the better.

Recognise that it may take time to adjust to being an ex-wife, and equally, it may not. As with the rest of your divorce, remain open to what is and remember that now you are an ex-wife, you are free to make your own decisions about your own life without an uninvited commentary from your ex-husband. Remember, too, that this cuts both ways – his life is now his business and, unless something that either of you do **negatively** impacts the children, it's not your concern. This can take practice!

Co-dependency

Perhaps your relationship with your husband was characterised by co-dependency. Co-dependency is where the dependant's behaviour is enabled and exacerbated by the other partner. If you're a 'helper' or a 'fixer' and you get your emotional needs met by doing good for others, at the detriment of your own needs, you may have co-dependence issues. If you or your husband believe that the other is there to 'make me happy', if one or both of you try to control situations and thoughts (mildly), you may have issues with co-dependency.

Co-dependency is tricky to overcome, but it is possible. Co-dependants tend to stay in relationships far longer than they know they should. They worry about how they will cope without the other person or they worry that the other person will be lost without them.

If this is you, be mindful of how you and your ex-husband communicate with each other. Be mindful too of the time you spend together. What's the real story? If you want to hang out so much together, why did you split? If it's like you're still together but not, it's likely there are co-dependency issues. You can get help and support with this, but the first thing to do is begin to let go.

Making a decision to move on

Making a decision to move on is important once you're divorced if you haven't already done it. It's important that you check in with yourself about whether you really have moved on and you're not just paying lip service to it to appease others. To fully move on, you have to let go. Let go of all hurt, pain, anger and regrets that you may have. You can't change the past; you can only move forward. Making a decision to move on can include taking the learnings from that past relationship and dealing with any issues that need resolving, particularly before embarking on a new relationship. Moving on is a conscious decision as much as an unconscious one. You can decide when and how it happens. Unconsciously, you may have already moved on without realising.

If it takes you some time, just be patient with yourself. It's not a race and everyone is different. Nobody else is you living your life. Trust that you will know when you have moved on. You will feel lighter, happier, less angry, and less consumed by thoughts of the past.

Learn to be with you first

Getting to know yourself again after divorce can be an adventure! What are your goals and aspirations and how can you put them into practice? By creating a relationship with yourself, you give yourself the best chance of moving forward in a healthy way, creating the trust and boundaries that you need in order to create the life that you want, whether or not somebody else is in it.

Take some time to acknowledge that you did get through your divorce even though at times it might have been a struggle. Recognise your strength, tenacity and resilience. Make a list of all the great things about you. Personality traits, skills, values and beliefs – the things that make you you!

Maintain or create a new routine

Some people like lots of routine, others less so. But the truth is, most of us benefit from some form of routine. Getting back into your routine or creating a new one will help create stability and clarity. This is particularly important if you have children, and it will be beneficial for you too. So long as the routine suits you, it doesn't matter what it is.

It might be that you start to have more free time at the weekends if your children now spend part of each weekend or every other weekend with their father. Now you have time on your hands. What can you do that's just for you with this time? Sure, part of it might be going to the supermarket without the children because you know that you'll get the shopping done more quickly and save yourself a lot of money! But what I'm really talking about here is something that's fun or nurturing just for you. Remember that it doesn't need to cost a lot of money, and if you want and are able to treat yourself, do!

Conscious uncoupling

Since Gwyneth Paltrow and Chris Martin got divorced in 2016 it seems that conscious uncoupling has become 'de rigueur'. Conscious uncoupling is a process popularised by Katherine Woodward Thomas which includes the philosophy that parents should separate amicably and keep up connection and communication for the sake of their children. This is not a new concept. Lawyers, family mediators and psychologists have said this for years. It forms the basis of any family separation. What makes conscious uncoupling different is the idea that there will be an active determination to keep some form of family unit together in the form of both parents sharing time together with their children regularly. Great. Right? Well, that depends on the real reason you do it, and the impact on you and the children.

For couples in a co-dependent relationship, this can exacerbate the problem because you don't move on. The end of a relationship is known as a 'separation'. Separation means the splitting of two things that were once connected. When conscious uncoupling occurs, separation isn't always clear. This is particularly true when one party doesn't want the separation. It's easy for them to get carried along in the fantasy that the relationship will continue. Without clear boundaries, moving on does not occur.

Separation is painful. Whether the separation was a joint decision or not. You have to go through the process, and the sooner you go through it, the sooner you can move forward with your life. Conscious uncoupling can be a way of delaying the inevitable. Spending lots of time together as friends for the sake of your kids is one thing, but the truth is, lots of people use this 'reason' in order to keep in close contact with their ex-partner. All is hunky-dory until, boom, one of you gets a new partner. Then all hell breaks loose. One of you feels betrayed, angry and hurt because now there is someone taking time and attention. The grieving process can then begin.

Adjusting to the role of co-parent takes time, space and practice. Allow yourself the opportunity to work through your separation.

Remember too that your children can be confused by it. Your separation is hard for your children. You know that. But the greatest gift you can give them is the message that Mummy and Daddy are not a couple any more. By spending lots of time together, you may confuse your children. Children are very definite. Things are black and white. They don't understand grey. Help your children cope by giving them black and white, at least for a while. Let them know that they have two homes. One with Mummy and one with Daddy. These are separate.

Separation should bring clarity to both parties and their children. "Mummy and Daddy don't live together. We are with Daddy on these days at these times and we are with Mummy on these days and times" gives everyone the clarity and certainty they need to adjust to a new way of living. Spending too much time together as your original family unit can blur that clarity.

It doesn't have to last forever, and in truth, the quicker your family can move forward in its new form, the sooner spending time together with your children can be a reality that benefits all of you.

Conscious uncoupling doesn't allow for a 'clean break'. I'm not talking about the financial 'clean break', I'm talking about the emotional one that cannot happen when boundaries are blurred. Does it mean you should never hang out as a family? No, absolutely not! But a clean break gives you and your children clarity. It's easier for children to cope with changes of routine when they can be sustained.

In many ways, conscious uncoupling is a great idea. You get to support your children and co-parent them together, showing that you are united as a family in its wider sense. However, initially, a clean break allows you time and space to adjust to the emotional and physical changes in your relationship.

This doesn't mean that your children don't see the parent who no longer lives at home; it means that until you have adjusted as a family to the changes, you don't hang out together as a family. Think about the strategies that will give you the best chance of moving forward in a way that's definite, clear and sustainable. Your children will thank you for it.

What if you don't divorce straight away?

Many people separate and don't get divorced straight away. This can be for a number of reasons. Some want to wait for two years' because divorcing by mutual consent feels right for them, others because they're not sure if this really is it, and others because they can't for financial or other reasons.

Some women are fine with this arrangement and others find it stressful. Financial uncertainty and a feeling that they're still being controlled. Remember that when you do get divorced, your financial circumstances in the here and now are the relevant ones. If you've been separated a while, this may come as a shock if you discover that money has been spent without your knowledge. This can still be taken into consideration on settlement but it's advisable, if you are going to be separated for a while, that you wrap up as many of the financial issues as you can and you're clear about what assets there are and where they are!

If you are struggling emotionally with this set-up, remember that you always have the choice to issue proceedings.

New relationships

A new relationship may be the last thing on your mind right now, but it could be one of a number of factors that has led you to be a lady who wants to leave. Whether you're ready for a new relationship right now or not, taking some time just to reflect on what that might look like and what's important for you in a new relationship can support you in making good choices in the future.

Remember that a new relationship won't deal with the issues of the past. If issues from your personal life and marriage are unresolved, you'll just be taking them with you into your new relationship. If you continue to do the same thing, expect to get the same result.

If you don't love yourself, no one else can. It really is as simple as that. Do you attract men who treat you badly? Do you attract good men whom you treat badly? If either one of these ladies is you, I invite you to work on loving yourself first. Go back to Section 1 where I talk about affirmations, and re-read the above paragraphs on co-dependency. Know that you can change your pattern of behaviour so that your next relationship is healthy for you, him and your children.

Often the issues that were a feature of your marriage will continue because they're just a part of life – washing, ironing, taxi service for the children – but what can be different this time?

When you do meet someone new, keep this relationship off Facebook. Even if your children are too young to have accounts of their own, they'll know someone who does. Posting about new relationships causes harm and increases tension which can escalate your legal bills. So before you post, think!

Introducing children to a new partner

As a family mediator and friend to several separated men and women, if there's one topic that hurts more than anything, it's the idea of children being introduced to a new partner. It can be hard, when you don't want to think of your children spending time with another woman. It can become the elephant in the room, so address it. There is nothing in law to stop this happening. Common sense is the way forward. This is where the Parenting Plan and family mediation can really help you.

If you haven't met new partners, where you can, agree in advance how the situation will be handled. It's not just about the number of months you've been dating or the fact that for you it's getting serious – it's about the readiness of the children to cope with it.

At best, agree that you'll tell the other parent as soon as you start dating someone with whom you think there may be a future, so that they are aware. As your relationship progresses, discuss with the other parent *how* and *when* the children will be told about the new person. If the other parent knows it's happening, they can then be prepared to answer questions and talk about it without feeling shocked or angry that they didn't know.

Remember that you can't control what the other parent does, and they can't control what you do. Be respectful and put the needs of your children first.

If the deed has already been done, and your children have been introduced to a new partner without your knowledge, well, don't let it eat you up. Where possible, use the Parenting Plan to agree how issues as large as this one are handled in the future, including any further relationships. Remember that children don't need to be introduced to every person you date, only those who have been in your life for some time and are likely to remain so.

Children may react badly to your new relationship, and do all they can to sabotage it, particularly if they want you and their father to get back together. Whilst this can be tricky, it is normal. Ensure that you make plenty of time for your children (it may mean more time than normal), as feelings of insecurity and sadness may increase. Let your children know that you still love them. Be mindful too that your children may well worry about their father when you get a new partner. They may think he'll be upset and lonely (he might). Be sensitive to this possibility. Your children, on the other hand, might be delighted that you're in a new relationship. You know your children best; putting them first will ensure that you support them as much as you can.

And finally ....

Thoughts of a family lawyer

Chris Myles is an experienced family lawyer, mediator, collaborative lawyer, head of department and director at Crombie Wilkinson LLP in York.

Here's what he'd like to say to ladies who leave...

Consider your husband's view

"It's likely that much of what you feel, your husband will too. He may lash out in anger or be abusive. He may fear losing his wife, his home, his children, his loss of standing in the community and self-worth. He may feel like a failure as a husband and father. You may think 'Why should I care?' Well, if he's feeling these things he may react. Try to let things go within reason. Avoid fueling the fire. Acknowledging these emotions often means that they sort themselves out.

"Temporary point scoring feels good in the short-term, but the damage can last forever..."

So what about the Ladies Who Left?

Angela

Angela and Michael reached agreement. Angela was able to remain in the family home with their daughter and Michael lives close by. He sees their daughter regularly, and when she's older she'll be able to take herself to his house. Angela and Richard are still together. Richard is having a challenging time in his divorce, but the two of them are looking forward to a future together.

Katie

Katie and Will have been separated for six months. Katie is exploring how collaborative law can support both her and Will to reach an agreement about their complex financial situation, in the most cost-effective way possible. It's likely that there are challenging times ahead for Katie, but she is determined as far as possible to keep the focus on resolving matters as swiftly and amicably as possible and ensuring that the children are protected.

Yvonne

Yvonne moved out of the family home some nine months ago. She's much happier and more relaxed. She has no plans to issue divorce proceedings and prefers to wait until she and Ted have been separated two years. She's hoping that Ted will be amenable to consenting to divorce at that stage and in the meantime, the two of them can agree a financial plan that will work for them both.

The last word ...

A word about men and divorce. If you're a man who has read this book – hello to you! Rest assured that my advice, if I'd written this book for you, would be exactly the same.

Not all ex-partners are a nightmare. Remember that the divorces you hear about on the television or you read about in the media are the stories that make us wince, gasp or plain laugh out loud. They aren't the run-of-the-mill divorce cases that occur every day.

Not every man runs off with his secretary leaving his wife penniless, just like not every woman wants to take her husband for every penny – if you were hoping that you'd get that advice in this book, I'm sorry I've disappointed you.

You see, whether you're a lady who leaves or a guy who's gone, it is possible to end your marriage with kindness, compassion and dignity. It's possible to divorce without destroying each other emotionally and financially and it is possible to move forward to be the healthy, happy person you are inside.

About Emma Heptonstall - The Divorce Alchemist

Image Olivia Brabbs Photography www.oliviabrabbs.co.uk

Emma Heptonstall is a former lawyer now practising family mediation and divorce coaching. She specialises in supporting Ladies Who Leave to make smart emotional and financial decisions at the end of their marriages.

Emma wrote this book to inspire you, the lady who is leaving, to take steps to move forward with courage and confidence.

Emma is a certified MBit Coach, NLP Master Practitioner and the author of *Understanding Divorce – 30 Daily Lessons*. She has featured in *Marie Claire*, the *Telegraph*, and is a regular contributor to *MeMeMe.online* and *Huffington Post*.

Having trained as a barrister and undertaken an LLM in Medical Ethics, Emma joined the Courts Service and spent 13 years as a legal adviser. In the latter part of her career, she trained in NLP and coaching for pleasure and began to use these techniques to great effect with families experiencing the challenges of relationship breakdown.

Having decided to train as a family mediator, Emma left the legal profession and began her career as a family mediator, whilst also setting up her coaching practice. It was at this point that Emma began to niche her coaching to divorcing women, and Divorce Alchemy was born.

Emma has coached ladies from around the world including Vietnam, South Africa and the United States, and works via Skype and FaceTime.

Contact Emma

Find out more about Emma and her coaching at
www.emmaheptonstall.com.

Glossary

Acknowledgement of service Document completed by the respondent to acknowledge receipt of the divorce petition and confirm whether divorce is accepted or contested.

Arbitration Alternative Dispute Resolution. Similar to mediation except the arbitrator has power to make a binding order.

Bailiff Responsible for enforcing court orders and the service of documents.

Bankruptcy Legal status denoting insolvency. Lasts 12 months on average. Clears debts but should be considered a last resort.

Cafcass Children and Family Court Advisory and Support Services –supporting and protecting children and families.

Capital Gains Tax (CGT) The tax to be paid when you sell an asset that has risen in value.

Certificate of service Legal document showing that one party has sent documents to another party.

Child arrangements order Children Act orders governing where a child shall live and who they spend time with. Formerly known as contact and residence orders.

Co-dependency The emotional or psychological over-dependence on another person, place or thing.

Collaborative law Divorce process where couples and their lawyers meet to negotiate an out-of-court settlement on divorce. Other professionals may also assist.

Consent order Order of the court which the parties have agreed.

Decree absolute This is the final court order bringing the marriage to an end.

Decree nisi A provisional order showing that the court is satisfied that the grounds for divorce have been established.

Domestic abuse Abuse that takes place in an intimate or family relationship which may be physical, emotional, psychological or financial.

Domicile The domicile of origin is normally where you are born unless a new domicile of choice is adopted by taking up permanent residence in another country.

Earmarking A method of setting aside part of a pension to be awarded to a spouse on the policy holder's retirement. Not much used now.

Family mediation Voluntary process of discussing family disputes with an independent third party.

Financial dispute resolution appointment Under present financial procedures, this is the second court appointment when the judge considers all offers made including those on a without prejudice basis.

Financial remedy order Financial order dealing with financial claims on divorce.

Financial disclosure Process of sharing financial information.

Final hearing Contested hearing where the case is before a judge to make a determination on the issues and make orders following.

First appointment The first court meeting when the judge considers what other information is needed to determine financial matters.

Form E The paperwork dealing with financial disclosure.

Habitually resident The place where you live.

IDVA Independent Domestic Violence Advisor – supporting men and women who experience domestic abuse through the legal process.

IVA Individual Voluntary Arrangement – a formal agreement to pay creditors some or all of the debt owed. If payments are not made, you could be made bankrupt.

MARAC Multi-Agency Risk Assessment Conference including health and social workers, police, housing and child protection officers.

Marriage certificate Legal document proving marriage.

Matrimonial Causes Act 1973 Legislation governing the court's powers on divorce.

Memorandum of Understanding (MOU) Document drawn up at the conclusion of mediation outlining the agreements and intentions made by the parties – not legally binding.

MIAM Mediation Information and Assessment Meeting – must be attended by the applicant for any financial order or order in respect of children.

Notice of disassociation A request to sever the financial links you may have with someone including a spouse due to joint credit, mortgage or bank account.

Parenting plan A written plan drafted by separating or divorcing parents to deal with the practical aspects of parenting. Can include anything the parents or children feel is important.

Pension sharing A method of sharing the pension of a spouse such that part of the pension becomes yours immediately (you don't necessarily have access to it).

Petitioner The person applying for a divorce.

Process server Similar to court bailiffs but are not employed by the court – authorised by law to serve papers upon another.

Public funding Legal aid. State funded legal representation.

Relate counselling National relationship and sex counselling organisation.

Respondent The spouse receiving the divorce papers.

Resources

It's my intention that *How to be a Lady Who Leaves* remains a resource that you can return to again and again. For this reason, and to ensure accuracy, many of the things you might want to know have been omitted from the book on purpose. Instead, you will find more resources to accompany the book at bit.ly/ Howtobealadywholeavesbookresources There you will also find details of how to book a 90-minute coaching session with me at a discount as a thank you for buying this book and to help you with your divorce journey.

» For general support with legal issues, debt management, housing and a wide range of personal and consumer issues: **Citizens Advice Bureau** www.citizensadvice.org.uk

» For lone parent support online and in national groups: **Gingerbread** www.gingerbread.org.uk

» For advice, support and tools for managing your money, dealing with debt, budget planners and much more: **Money Advice Service** www.moneyadviceservice.org.uk

» To find a family mediator in your area: **Family Mediation Council** www.familymediationcouncil.org.uk or **Resolution** (see below).

» To find a family lawyer who will support you to reach a negotiated settlement and avoid lengthy court proceedings: **Resolution** www.resolution.org.uk

» To download all the up-to-date court forms:
Gov.uk www.gov.uk

» To find support for domestic abuse issues where you can delete your browsing history:
Women's Aid www.womensaid.org.uk
or **Refuge** www.refuge.org.uk (also offers support for men who experience abuse).

» For information about options in relation to your pension:
The Pension Advisory Service www. pensionsadvisoryservice.org.uk

» To change your name by Deed Poll:
www.gov.uk/changing-passport-information/ name-divorce-deed-poll-forenames-title

» To change the details on your driving licence:
https://www.gov.uk/change-name-driving-licence

Lightning Source UK Ltd.
Milton Keynes UK
UKOW06f1924130617
303167UK00001B/201/P